Astrology & Profession

Astrology & Profession

Astrological Principles Behind Career Selection, Downfall and Resurrection

Author

Ajay Srivastava

First Edition, 2025

Published by:

Ajay Kumar Srivastava

45, Awas Vikas Colony, Betiya Hata,

Gorakhpur – 273001 (U.P.), India

Mobile No.: +91-9867837184

Lord Ganesha

Prayer

ॐ नमो सिद्धि विनायकाय सर्व कार्य कर्त्रे सर्व विघ्न प्रशमनाय

सर्व राज्य वश्यकरणाय सर्वजन सर्वस्त्री पुरुष आकर्षणाय

श्रीं ॐ स्वाहा ।।

|| Om Namo Siddhi Vinayakaya Sarva kaarya kartrey Sarva vighna prashamnay Sarvarjaya Vashyakarnaya Sarvajan Sarvastree Purush Aakarshanaya Shreeng Om Swaha ||

(**Translation**: O Lord of Wisdom and Happiness, only you make every endeavor and everything possible. You are the remover of all obstacles and you have enchanted every being in the Universe, you are the Lord of all women and all men, amen.)

Dedication

I dedicate this book to my father (Late) Sri Ram Ashrey Lal Srivastava who taught me to be an independent, courageous and determined person, and my mother Maya Srivastava whose unconditional love and support always help me to overcome all the obstacles in my life. She has a selfless spirit and served others throughout her life. Her immense patience is peerless and she always inspires me to go ahead.

Preface

Every person wants continuous success and prosperity in life. It is a common tendency of a person to get greedy for things that are available without any effort. So, free things always attract but success in life is never free. We have to work hard at every step and only those who walk on this path know its real value. Long-lasting success demands effort, dedication, and hard work. Every step takes our energy and time that can never be gained.

So, we should take our steps carefully and every step taken towards a career is important because it decides the direction of whole life. Therefore, it is very important to choose the right direction because in the present time there is a lot of confusion.

People start following successful people around them but after some time they realize that they are on the wrong path. By then they have put a lot of time and energy and if they do not get positive results, then they start getting disappointed. Astrology helps us in choosing the right career by recognizing the qualities inside us.

The path of life is not always even and there are many ups and downs in it. When the direction of life is upward then people are happy but when odd circumstances start then they start blaming others. They start blaming their advisors, family members, and friends but never blame themselves.

On the uncertain paths of life, the knowledge of astrology can help to move ahead on the unknown path, but it is the responsibility of the individual to move ahead and work hard to achieve success. When a stone is seen on the way, it is the responsibility of the person himself to remove it, and not to blame others. But people only want to hear about success and when difficulties come in their way they are quick to blame others.

Astrology is the science of understanding the effects of the invisible rays of planets and stars upon us and with the help of this science, people try to know what is written in fate and what is pulling us towards?

How do these invisible rays have the power to decide the direction of our life? The knowledge of astrology helps us understand all these things, but we should remember that the future is always in the hands of God.

This book explains the characteristics of all nine planets and the effects of these planets on different professions. It explains about service and business and how to choose a specific profession. This book also explains the ups and downs of a career, astrological combinations for its downfall, and how to deal with these difficult situations in life.

In this book, I have taken some material from my previous books, and have also added some material, because the matter of profession and downfall is very wide and involves many aspects of life.

I bow down to God for completing this book. Without the grace of the Almighty, it is not possible for me to express my thoughts in words.

Ajay Srivastava

September 18, 2024

Acknowledgement

The existence of this book would not have been possible without the help of my wife Seema and my daughter Saanvi. They provided me enough help to write down my thoughts which I have collected so far in my life. My wife has been instrumental as an illustrator and proof-reader and has given me enough insights to write the matter in a simple and explanatory manner.

Ajay Srivastava

Contents

Chapter 1

Introduction

Planets and Nakshatras affect human life as well as our profession. Every person has to choose a profession for his livelihood and it depends on his skills and abilities. Parents send their children to schools and colleges to develop skills as nature supports learning in this stage of life. Children learn quickly, so Mercury in astrology represents skills and childhood status.

Parents are always curious to know what their children will become when they grow up and what profession they will take up. Therefore, the choice of profession becomes very important. However, once a profession is chosen it is not necessary that a person stays in the same profession for life. Due to the various options available and the rapidly changing economic scenario, changing professions has now become a common thing. People often ask whether they will do a job or a business and which profession will be better for them. Today in the age of technology and due to the changing political scenario globally, employment and business get badly affected. Jobs that were available a few years ago are no longer available and many businesses are severely affected.

Layoffs are common and often we hear such news. Therefore, people are scared about the future of their career because when the source of income stops the mind also stops working and some people are not able to face the adverse circumstances of life and some of them take wrong steps. Our life provides many types of good and bad experiences and all of them together give birth to a very mature and unwavering person. A strong person is one who does not bow down to adversity, who struggles and overcomes the storms and stress of life.Advancement in life is not easy and cheap, it comes through voluntary and persistent effort.

The Sun provides the strength to fight all obstacles in life. A strong Sun indicates vigour and vitality and such a person never bows down to circumstances. The Sun is the source of light. As soon as the Sun comes, darkness disappears as if it never existed. Sun means moving forward and pushing back the darkness. If a person surrenders to the darkness of life then his Sun becomes weak. The one who fights with darkness, his Sun becomes strong and one day light is born within him.

That is why a person should never surrender to darkness. That is why suicide is considered a sin in every religion. The person who deliberately gave up the search for light and succumbed to darkness, weakened his Sun. He has given birth to cowardice within himself. The one who searches for light never succumbs to darkness. Darkness can never be so powerful that it can bend the light because no matter how long the night is, morning always comes and this is the eternal truth.

I learned that if one door closes, another opens. But if a person is knocking on the door due to some external influence without realizing his own potential, then the chances of such a door opening are very less. In such a situation, astrology helps in choosing the right direction for career by recognizing our inner nature. It helps in identifying the areas where you can focus your energy.

Jupiter is the planet that brings expansion in our lives. To be lucky in your endeavors, one needs the strength of Jupiter. The presence of Jupiter indicates that the person gets expansion easily in matters related to that house. But when a person starts getting things easily in life, bad habits start taking birth in him. Where the activity of expansion is involved, it should be controlled, otherwise it creates many evils.

People do not value whatever comes easily in life. They forget to set limits in their activities of expansion and when things cross their limits the result of a benefic planet becomes negative. The ancient sutra (Sthan Hani Karo Jeeva) says that Jupiter harms the place where it is placed and this is true if we forget to set limits. For example, excessive consumption of sugar can alter the taste buds. Excessive speed can cause accidents, so brakes are necessary.

Venus signifies freshness, the ability to understand subtle things, and the ability to work flawlessly. It is not possible to reach the top in just one or two attempts. A person climbing to the top fails many times, but the desire to reach the heights always call him. Venus being exalted in Pisces indicates this because tireless efforts are required to transform sexual energy into spiritual energy. Venus symbolizes the highest level of perfection; hence, the gemstone of Venus is diamond. After years of pressure and heat, ordinary coal turns into precious diamond.

Saturn is the lord of karma and gives pressure and heat with the aim that one day the person will become like a diamond. It creates obstacles and hindrances in life. Saturn forces the person to work hard and teaches him to be patient in life as it takes millions of years to turn coal into a diamond. Every pressure given by Saturn is a process of conversion. Saturn acts as a cleaner and cleans everything that has become garbage in our lives. But people get attached to their garbage and are not ready to remove it from their lives.

When garbage accumulates on the road and the cleaner does not come, then after a few days it becomes impossible to walk. The working style of Saturn is also similar to that of the garbage cleaner. When garbage accumulates everywhere, life becomes difficult, diseases start spreading, and progress stops. Therefore, for development, it is necessary to remove the garbage first. Development cannot happen without removing the garbage, whether it is a house or a city or a country.

The same principle applies to every person's life as well. Without removing the garbage, no one can move forward in life, and due to our ignorance, pebbles and garbage get collected, so cleanliness is necessary for development.

Saturn is harsh and shows no mercy when the question of removal of waste comes, without which there is no growth. Therefore, the ancient sutra (Sthan Vridhi Karo Shani) is right about Saturn that where it is placed, it increases the results of that place by removing all the dirt of that place.

The position of Saturn in the horoscope indicates that there is a lot of scope for progress in that place, but hard work is required. Saturn never gives any fruit without hard work. The position of Saturn also indicates that we should be ready to work hard as there are many hurdles to cross. When one gets success after hard work then happiness is something else and this is a real success. Therefore;

- Saturn represents pressure and pain and Venus represents pleasure and happiness.
- Saturn represents hard work and Venus represents celebration.
- Saturn is stubborn and Venus is tender but they both are friends.
- Saturn is a cruel planet. On one hand, it blocks the path and on the other hand, it removes unnecessary rocks so that water can flow easily.

The nature of water is to flow but it cannot remove the stone coming in its way. It needs the help of Saturn who is ruthless in putting and throwing stones. Venus is delicate, sensitive, and represents fresh water. Venus needs the strong and firm hands of Saturn to achieve its purpose just like water needs the support of rocks to flow in a direction. Therefore, it is impossible for Venus to achieve anything without the help of Saturn. Saturn makes way for Venus which represents ultimate achievement, but a weak Venus indicates that the native seeks sensual pleasures and often attends parties without making any effort.

The transit of Saturn plays an important role in life. Saturn removes every adulteration, every falsehood, and every garbage then only the truth remains. Saturn clears every unnecessary thing in life. That is why it is said that Saturn clears away all the dirt and shows the real truth to the person.

Today, this human body which is liked by many people, but a day will come when no one will like it. One day it will turn into waste and people will throw it in the crematorium and burn it like garbage. When Saturn transits on the ascendant it gives disease, it means that some part of the body has become waste and one day the whole body will become waste. Every waste has to be thrown away, but people form attachment to their garbage and do not want to remove it. They keep collecting it for years but they do not know that it has become a burden for their development.

Saturn throws away all the garbage and has to use force if the person is not ready to leave it. So, Saturn is harsh because it does not allow any kind of garbage to be kept in our lives. When Sade Sati starts people start getting scared because they are not ready to throw away their garbage and the conflict starts. They keep collecting it for years and think that there are valuable things in their collection. But Saturn does not allow to keep anything that has become waste.

So, Saturn removes the ego in Sade Sati because it is completely useless but people are not ready to throw it away. Then Saturn uses force and removes the cause of ego, so, people lose wealth, power, and position in their Sade Sati. The transit of Saturn clears everything, the waste has gone and now life can move forward (Sthan Vridhi Karo Shani).

Mars provides energy to achieve the goal and the Moon represents our mind. Everything in this world is a play of our mind. When the mind stops, everything stops, so the position of the Moon plays an important role in making any decision in life.

In astrology, the horoscope is divided into two axes - day (above the horizon) and night (below the horizon) hemispheres. The first house to the seventh house is called the day part or upper half. Strong planets placed above the horizon in the horoscope indicate the popularity and prosperity of the person. It indicates the external focus like professional achievement and interpersonal relationships. Planets placed below the horizon indicate the internal focus of the person like domestic environment, self, family, creativity, etc. Planetary transit plays a vital role in determining the favorable time. Planning to change your career (from job to business and vice versa) depends on your planetary position, dasha, and transit. Your horoscope is your secret that helps you to discover your talent and avoid making wrong decisions.

"There is no better boat than a horoscope to help a man cross over the sea of life." - Varaha Mihira

Chapter 2

The Zodiac

Not every place on earth is the same, some places have fresh water and some places have swamps and seas. Some places have abundant greenery, fertile land and some places are deserts where there is no trace of water anywhere. Some places have fires burning all the time and some places have snowy mountains. Some places are extremely dangerous where people never think of going and some places are extremely beautiful and people like to go there again and again. This is our earth where diversity exists everywhere.

Our ancient scriptures say that even the sky above us is not the same. Astrology has divided the sky into 4 elements and 12 zodiac signs and each zodiac sign is related to some element. These elements are - fire, earth, air and water. Knowledge of these elements and zodiac signs plays an important role in decision making as they deeply influence the personality and behavior of every individual. Before delving deeper into astrology, it is important to understand the qualities of each zodiac sign.

Table: Sign, Element, and Quality

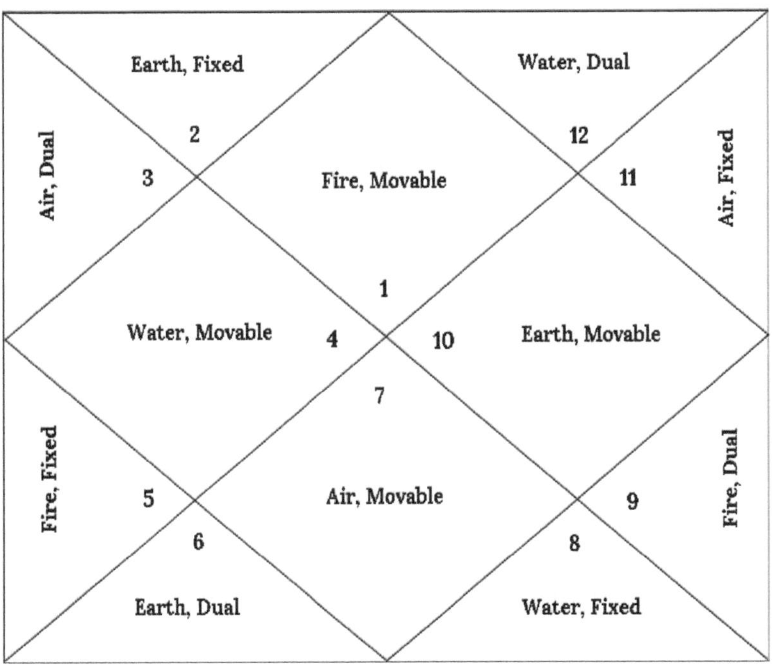

2.1 Four Elements

2.1.1 Fire - Aries, Leo, Sagittarius

Every fire sign marks the beginning of a new cycle. After every four zodiac signs a Gandanta exists where the water ends and fire begins, so fire signifies a new beginning. These people are initiative takers and do not hesitate to take immediate action. They do not mind burning their fingers but they cannot sit silently and wait for safety. They are courageous people who step into the unknown, no matter what the outcome, they are risk-takers and always stand ahead of others.

- Fire signifies enthusiasm and passion. Hence, these people are dynamic individuals and never shy away from taking the first step.

- Fire indicates action and movement. They are leaders and pioneers and can provide direction to others.

- Fire indicates transformation, purification, and a desire for knowledge. They are seekers of wisdom and love to read books and discuss intellectual matters.

It requires caution when handling fire and this is a masculine and active energy. They never retrace their steps because the direction of fire is always upward. They are the best where action and initiation are required, they are the initiators.

On the other hand, they are impatient and jump into action without proper thinking. It is not good to play with fire, it burns. They are angry people and can explode at any time.

2.1.2 Earth - Taurus, Virgo, Capricorn

Earth sign indicates practical and grounded person. They are very hard-working people and always follow every order diligently. They are dutiful person and finish their job without any complaints. Earth indicates receptivity and patience; hence these people analyze every fact and figure before making any decision. They seek prosperity and work hard to improve and secure their financial position.

- Earth signs represent loyalty, trust, responsibility, and morality.

- Earth signs represent a strong conviction. They are determined people who are true to their words.

- Earth provides stability. They are a peace-loving person and prefer stability in their life. They are never in a hurry and do everything with full dedication. They are the best person for desk work, documentation, and for those work where stability is the top priority.

These people are not suitable for those work where action and initiation are required. No one can question that they have not completed their work on time, but they are unable to take initiative like the fire signs people. This is because these are feminine and passive energies. Therefore, security comes first and these people prefer the middle path in their lives. They look for stability first and move forward when everything is secure.

On the other hand, they are rigid individuals who do not like to change anything. They stick to their old thoughts and believe that they are always right. Because they always prefer stability, they reject new ideas and thoughts and prefer to stay in their safe cell. They do not accept revolutionary ideas and are unable to adjust to the changing environment.

2.1.3 Air - Gemini, Libra, Aquarius

Air indicates freedom, when air circulates, it is fresh, and when it gets stuck in a place, it starts giving a foul smell. Therefore, these people lack stability, are unable to sit in one place, and prefer to wander here and there.

They are the best person for marketing, public relations, and networking-related jobs.

They are an intelligent person with strong analytical abilities. They are witty individuals and are strong in communication. They are thinkers, who analyze the situation and probe deeply.

- Air spreads, so they prefer wandering. They are ready to move anytime and like to travel.

- Air is a mixture of many gases. They have complex minds, able to do mental calculations, and understand the complexity of the issue quickly.

- Air is invisible, swift, and elusive. It is difficult to read the minds of these people. Their ideas are invisible to others. They are smart people, who know how to quickly do their work and disappear.

Air is everywhere, we draw air in and out of our bodies. This process goes on continuously even without our knowledge. Hence, these signs can perform their work silently without getting noticed by others. All means of communication belong to the air signs. Just like deep breathing keeps a person calm, similarly the air signs have the immense ability to generate new and innovative thoughts to make life better.

On the other hand, fraudsters, cheaters, and scammers fall under these signs, they use their skills to deceive others. They are selfish people and use their minds only to fulfill their desires and disappear quickly like air. They are smart people to hide their identity from all these nefarious activities. They believe that just like the air cannot be caught, they too cannot be caught; the air is invisible so no one can know their true identity.

2.1.4 Water - Cancer, Scorpio, Pisces

Water sign people are very sensitive, emotional, and moody. They are not rigid as water changes its shape quickly. Their intuition is very strong as water picks up vibrations quickly. Water has nurturing qualities so they are helpful people and take care of others. These people are deeply connected to emotions. They like to get involved in activities where emotions matter and understanding through observation is important. Because of their keen instincts they can understand the intentions of others. They are keen observers and can understand hidden motives and body language instantly.

Nurturing qualities are important for these people. They are quick to rush to help others when called upon. Hence, they are suitable for social work, hospitality, fiction writing, penetration and discovery of secrets, etc. As they have high sensitivity they are interested in art and music. They can feel the vibrations happening with the person or in the environment around them.

- Water has the unique ability to dissolve substances. These people easily mingle with others in any situation without complaining.

- Water evaporates due to heat. However, at first, they try to tolerate what they do not like but when the situation creates excessive heat they leave that place forever.

- Water signs are like tidal waves. These people are ready to create strong bonds but can also create havoc once in a while when the energy of hidden feelings becomes very high.

The heat capacity of water is very high due to hydrogen bonding among water molecules. It takes a lot of energy to increase its temperature by one degree. Therefore, water prevents the heat from getting absorbed into the environment and helps in controlling the temperature. Therefore, these people are cool-minded individuals and forgive others easily.

On the other hand, they care too much about others and ignore their own needs. They are generous people and sometimes others try to take undue advantage of their generosity. They are highly emotional and feel hurt easily. They are unable to face the negativity of life and start crying easily. They are fickle-minded people and their mood keeps changing constantly.

2.2 Qualities of Signs

There are three types of qualities - Movable, Fixed and Dual (Common or Mutable).

2.2.1 Movable Signs - Aries, Cancer, Libra, Capricorn

As the name suggests, these people easily adapt to new situations and find their own way out of a problem rather than waiting for a person or a particular time. They like change, take initiative and encourage others. They are goal-oriented individuals and flow with purpose in life. They accept challenges and look for new opportunities instead of holding back.

The movable sign indicates a new beginning and their every beginning begins with change. Like a new season begins but it is the end of the previous season. This indicates that they are leaders and trendsetters who remove old things and implement new changes.

But every change carries some risk and if the person is not able to assess it, the result creates problems for many people. Therefore, they are visionary individuals who properly understand the risks involved in the task. As the seasons change with the movement of the Sun, they implement new ideas and bring about change.

On the other hand, it indicates an impulsive and dissatisfied person who takes worthless initiatives, is restless and gets easily agitated. They waste their energy in worthless wandering and ultimately get no results.

2.2.2 Fixed Signs - Taurus, Leo, Scorpio, Aquarius

They are stable and consistent people. They are loyal and remain firm on their decisions. They believe in their tradition and do not like change. Their nature is to do everything fix, so that there is no further risk. They are perfectionists, work hard and complete tasks with utmost dedication. They do not like anything half-baked, be it work or relationship, and when the reaction of the other person is lackluster, they leave it forever.

They know how to maintain things and keep things safe but they are unable to take initiation. They like to follow the action plan without any change, prioritize safety first and prefer to stay in the middle as there are chances of falling off to the side. Therefore, they choose only those options where the risk is minimal and no chance of any loss.

On the other hand, they are stubborn individuals who do not like to change their opinions. They also cling to negative things and find it very difficult to let them go.

2.2.3 Dual Signs - Gemini, Virgo, Sagittarius, Pisces

It is also known as common or mutable sign. The word dual means related to two. When two parts or aspects of something come together it indicates duality in their personality. This means that they can do two things at the same time. Like a chameleon changes its color according to the situation, although this is taken in a negative sense, but in other words it adapts itself to the situation without complaining. Therefore, these people adjust to the situation and have the ability to adapt quickly to changing circumstances without any complain. These qualities indicate that they are very flexible and versatile person.

The meaning of dual nature is neither mobile nor stable but it is a mixture of both and one of them comes out according to the circumstances. The changed behavior of the person may surprise others that what was previously static is now showing dynamic tendencies, but everything depends on the circumstances.

Therefore, these people immediately sense the change in circumstances even before it occurs and prepare everything in advance for safety, just like a chameleon changes its color quickly and is able to hide from the eyes of others.

On the other hand, they are able to hide their true face and can easily deceive others. It also shows the selfish nature of the person. The person who was very sociable at one time, his behavior suddenly changes and the second behavior is completely different from the previous one. Due to circumstances, his second aspect has now come to the surface and that is completely different from the first aspect.

2.3 Sun Ingress

Movable zodiac signs are initial signs, fixed zodiac signs come under the middle and dual zodiac signs indicate the end. The Sun enters Aries on 14 April and Pisces on 15 March and completes a cycle of rotation from movable sign to dual sign. When the Sun enters the movable (chara) sign, four seasons start respectively - spring, summer, autumn and winter.

Chapter 3

The Twelve Signs

In Vedic astrology, to know a person's zodiac sign we need to see in which sign his moon is placed. The moon represents the mind of a person, so it is important for the moon to be strong. A strong moon indicates that the person is not afraid of adversities in life, his mind remains calm and he takes decisions only after thorough consideration. A weak moon indicates that the person is easily afraid and surrenders to circumstances.

Understanding the different phases of the Moon is very important in astrology. When the Moon is exactly opposite the Sun (180° or 7th house) in a horoscope, it is a full moon day. Moon is considered weak within 72 degrees from the Sun. Amavasya (new moon) occurs when Sun and Moon both are in the same house and less than 13.2 degrees from each other.

3.1 Aries

Ariens aspire to be the head of all affairs and do not like subordination. If this sign is strong and receives beneficial aspects, then they have good commanding power and can provide proper direction to others. When they recognize the opportunity, they can move forward against all odds with confidence. They are impulsive and lack the quality of patience. They have quick reactions and are not afraid to play with sharp objects. They are not afraid to try new things, take on new challenges, and want to take on another task before completing the first one.

Being the first sign of the zodiac, they have leadership qualities and are willing to take the initiative. They are entrepreneurial by nature and always aim high. The first sign represents initiation and newness; hence, they are the initiator of new things and the founder of the organization. It takes courage, vision, and high energy to start anything new and Ariens have that type of quality. The first sign also represents birth, innocence, and the beginning of the journey. They prefer to travel alone and do not wait for their companions, friends, and followers.

Being a positive sign of Mars, this energy acts as a protector and they are the best people to deal with a situation like an emergency. They have a strong ability to understand human psychology and are well versed in research and invention. They are very observant and have a scientific and logical mind which is full of new ideas. Two other fire signs, Leo and Sagittarius are their best companions.

This sign represents strong self-confidence, a forceful character, a thrust for their goal, and an uncompromising soul. Being a positive sign, they are ready to forgive others, they are outspoken have a clean heart, and do not like circumrotating matters. They never surrender and keep fighting till the end, their motto is – “Success or death but no retreat”. Mars, the lord of Aries, also rules over Scorpio, which is eighth from here and is also the house of transformation. Therefore, Aries people’s life is not stable and they get to see many changes. Being adventurous people, they keep moving from one place to another in search of new experiences.

Affliction: If the sign is afflicted, they are arrogant, quarrelsome, fierce, and boisterous. If more malefic influences the sign, then this energy will convert into obsession and they are ready to fight with anyone to fulfill their desire. They are explosive and may outburst on any matter. They behave like an autocrat and are not ready to listen to anyone's advice.

3.2 Taurus

Taureans have their principles and follow a practical path in their life. They are very devoted people and follow their traditions. They are straightforward, reliable, loyal, and creative people. They are faithful, trustworthy, persistent, and stable people. They have a strong sense of humour and are fond of pleasure. They have a strong sense of responsibility and work very diligently.

The sensitivity of Taureans is very high. They are emotional, sober, and romantic people. They don't run after relationships, but once it's done, they hold them for a long time, and they keep their promises. It is a highly fertile sign and a planet posited in Taurus feels highly comfortable and its productivity is high. Like, Ketu in Taurus, the native's inclination is toward religion and spiritual activities, and the native can easily remember religious doctrines. Venus in Taurus, the native can excel in Venusian pursuits easily.

Taureans have patience, are very honest, and work very hard. They are those people who have the strong capability to complete the unfulfilled task and never leave anything in between but they lack the initiation and aggression of Aries - which is the first sign of the zodiac.

Taureans are easily motivated by Venusian pursuits and want to enjoy the fruits of their labour. They are motivated by happiness and pleasure and like to enjoy parties, marriages, and other gatherings. They are very generous and like to invite friends for dinners. They are very cautious about their diet and correct nutrition is their first choice. They love cooking and gardening and plant beautiful creepers, flowers, plants, and trees.

Due to the Venus-ruled sign, they have an attractive face and an inclination towards Venusian qualities like singing, music, dance, etc. They are dress cautious people and always prefer to wear good-looking clothes. They communicate very well and like comfort and luxury in their life.

Being the second sign of the zodiac, it represents face and expressions, etc. It is also a house of family, wealth, and worldly possessions. Therefore, they are good in business, understand money-related matters very quickly and work hard to accumulate property.

Taurus is a quadruped sign; therefore, their movement is slow and sometimes they take a long time to complete the task but when fully charged their capacity is very high from others to move forward. They are perfectionists and due to the strong quality of patience, they are not ready to compromise easily and work hard for perfection. They are very liberal and broad-minded people and always ready to help others and even sometimes they forget their own money given to some other person.

Being an earthy sign, they prefer stability and don't like sudden changes in their life. They are very cautious people and prefer to put their feet back where there is any kind of insecurity. They are a valuable asset to the organization but when the organization is not ready to provide the stability and proper security for their future, they have no hesitation to leave such places. Taureans don't prefer to take a risk and prefer security in their life. Therefore, they prefer to do secure jobs and the temptation of big money does not attract them.

Like valuable assets, they are valuable people to their surroundings. They believe in hard labour, but sometimes they are very stubborn, lazy, and resistant to change. Due to stubbornness, they don't bother about other person's opinions and they don't change their opinion to please others. Their anger comes very slowly but once they are raged it is very difficult to control them. Sometimes their attitude is very dogmatic, which can lead to fierce anger and ready to destroy any obstruction.

Affliction: If the sign is afflicted then the person will become lazy and does not listen even after shouting. They are pleasure-seeking people and can take any wrong path to fulfill their desire, like overindulgence in sexual activities, drugs, etc. They are reserved, conservative, and egoistic people. They are covetous, may indulge to attain only physical pleasure, and will not give heed to any advice. Sometimes they are outright challengers to elders and superiors.

3.3 Gemini

They are skilled persons and have a desire to create something new and explore new things. Mercury represents an intellectual personality with strong communication skills which can argue with logic and can offer his best advice. Being a dual sign, they are versatile. They are joyful but they are not easily satisfied and believe in change and in search of that they move from one place to another.

Geminis have sharp intelligence and their reaction is quick and witty. Being a dual sign, they can do more than one profession at a time. They are the person who can see both sides of the coin simultaneously. Therefore, they are best fitted with the job where negotiating skills are required. They are successful salespeople, brokers, and diplomats. They have a democratic attitude. The twin symbol indicates that they will perform better when they co-operate with others and will show their best performance when they undertake any job in co-operation. Gemini is all about output, so they express their feelings externally while Virgo - the other sign ruled by Mercury, processes their emotions internally. Geminis are interested in writing reviews, love to chat, and while speaking they use their hands frequently.

Mercury represents a child who has an interest in asking questions. Mercury represents a merchant with strong business acumen, a merchant who is always looking to strike a fair deal, a merchant who does not reject an offer and loves to discuss first. Mercury represents strong intelligence, clear and logical thinking, penetrating vision, strong retention power, impulsive action, etc., Geminis have all such qualities.

They enjoy business conversation and are tactfully able to convert matters in their favour. They are liberal on the one hand and frugal on the other, both peculiar qualities present in their personality. They are inquisitive, like intelligent discussion and good orators. They have excellent writing skills and talent in multiple languages. They are very curious people to seek all facts and figures before taking any action and keep asking questions till they get a clear idea to understand the matter. But sometimes, they behave like a highly timid and nervous person.

Gemini - The Twins, represents unification of masculine and feminine energy which gives birth to pure wisdom and provides immense possibilities for spirituality.

Affliction: They are a highly indecisive person and lack quality of concentration. They do not have patience and want to see the fruits of their work immediately. They are interested in shortcuts to achieve success and use their brain to dodge others. The shallow and wavering mind can convert into a cynic and eccentric person.

3.4 Cancer

Cancer is the first of the three water signs; its water is considered to be freshwater. Cancerians are very sensitive and emotional people. Just as a particle destroys the purity of water, they get easily hurt even by the loud voice of others. They are very kind and loving people but moody and peevish too. They are loyal and honest person. They are tenacious and feel strong bondage with their family and culture. They do not give up easily, once they have identified their goals.

People born under this sign have a strong memory and a powerful intuition. They are deep observant and notice everything. They cover every minor detail and don't overlook anything. They are mysterious people who are not ready to open up easily, and keep everything to themselves.

They prefer a safe environment, a peaceful home, and a family life. They are looking for security first under any circumstances and want to remain in their shell if they sense any sign of danger. They are shy, non-aggressive person and do not believe in any kind of violence. They have a great desire to nurture and grow themselves and others.

Water can assume any shape depending upon the vessel, so they adapt to any situation. Being feminine and watery sign, they are very productive and produce great results if utilize their talent properly. Like water is not compressible, cancer-born people become rebellious when someone puts pressure on them, then they become very determined, stubborn, and outrageous.

Moon is the ruler of the sign represents the nurturing quality of the person. They are great teachers like a mother and able to provide proper guidance to others. They have a quick grasping ability and can produce new and innovative ideas. Like the waxing and waning Moon, Cancerians witness remarkable changes in their life. Being a movable and watery sign, they lead a wandering and restless life, experiencing many things and feeling life very deeply.

As the satellite of earth (Moon) movement is very fast, they are restless in nature and impatient. The exaltation of Jupiter signifies the protective nature of the sign while debilitation of Mars signifies the non-combative nature and inaction of this sign.

Affliction: If the sign is afflicted, they never forget their enemies and wait patiently for the time to take revenge.

They are very cruel towards enemies. They are very talkative and fickle-minded people. They are unable to take timely decisions and keep important files for a long time due to indecision, many times they miss opportunities due to inaction and indecisiveness.

3.5 Leo

Leonians, being a sign of the Sun, have a great desire for creation and the will to live. There is no life on earth without Sun, when Sun rises darkness disappears. Worship of the Sun removes ignorance and evil thoughts. Leonians take very much interest in creative activities and join those organizations which are helpful to mankind. A positive, and fire sign represents thrust for knowledge and they are always ready to learn. They are frank and broad-minded person. On the other hand, they are blunt and outspoken, therefore, they have fewer friends.

Fire and fixed signs represent a high level of energy. They are like a young adult who has confidence in their ability and are ready for action. They are a warm, passionate and charismatic person. They are extroverts with full of fun. They have dignity, hate getting their hands dirty, and prefer to get others to do such kind of work. They are a very honest person and it is difficult to question their integrity. They are an intelligent and hard-working person and learn in art and culture. They want to live a free life and hate any kind of boundation.

Leonians are self-centered and ambitious people. They are choosy in relationships. Like a father protecting his family, they feel a responsibility to protect their surroundings. They help people voluntarily and do charity. They never hesitate to help their friends and are ready to give up their comfort when needed. Prestige and honour are of great importance for them and they are willing to maintain it at any cost even when they are in a state of scarcity. They are very cautious about their dress, curtains, and furniture and keep their home tidy. They are extravagant and want to live lavishly; therefore, they face tough times in life due to poor savings.

Planets in this sign represent the leadership quality of the person and a sense of showmanship. They have a desire to be seen and display their talent to the world. Planets in Leo represent a person who wants to be independent and attract attention, admiration, and respect from others. Sun in Leo represents that the person has leadership quality, fewer friends, and live a lonely life. Mountain or caves represents the isolation and silence of the sign. They do not talk much and hate worthless discussions. In a meeting at first, they hear every opinion and pay attention to every rumor and take judgment judiciously.

Sun always moves in forward motion and never retrogrades. They are known for their determination, bravery, loyalty, stability, and consistency.

Lions have terrific night vision and are most active at night; therefore, Leonians find themselves comfortable at night work without any sign of lethargy. Early morning wake-up is not a problem for Leonians. Lions are ready to fight to protect their food, so Leonians are ready to fight when needed. They lead a disciplined life and spend most of their lives in one place.

Affliction: If the sign is afflicted, they become highly arrogant and aggressive person. They are short-tempered and feel hurt by any trivial matter. They are conservative and stubborn; dormant and stupid; harsh and tough; tyrant and ruthless. They have an urge for recognition and an excessive desire to be special. Because of their pride, they are susceptible to flattery and by exaggerating their ego sycophants use this weakness.

3.6 Virgo

The rulership of Mercury represents an analytical mind, intelligence, and strong business acumen. This sign is capable of producing great business leaders but they also have to go through tough phases of life. They have strong potential for creation. They like to cooperate with others and are very good at teamwork. They use their intellect to win debates, good critics and are strong in negotiations. They have clear concepts and can present disorganized data in an organized manner. They want to finish one task first before starting other.

Mercury is also a fast-moving planet, which indicates inconsistency. They like to travel and move from their birthplace. They are quick in action and often change their residence and jobs. They are shy and sensible people. They are discerning, patient, careful, and meticulous people.

They are practical and detail-conscious people. They are soft-spoken people and always keep lovely smiles on their faces. They are a smart, active person and look younger than their age. They are conscious about their physique and keep control of their tummy.

Earthy signs represent reliability and stubbornness. They are hardworking and conscientious people. They keep a strong grip on their holding and take care of their belongings. They are good at saving money and their secret savings no one knows. They never reveal their secrets to anyone. They like gardening and agriculture.

Being a dual sign, they look for alternate possibilities and focus on alternate sources of income. They keep back up of their important items. They adjust themselves as per the situation when necessary. They are perfectionists, every task after completion they check it again which reduces the chances of mistakes and increases their perfection. As Leos prefer to show their talent to the world, Virgoans prefer to develop their talent, one after another. This is the sign where the best logical and spiritual exploration of the universe begins and they have an insatiable desire to quest for the truth.

Affliction: If the sign is afflicted, they are an argumentative and illicit pleasure-seeking person. They use their brain to take undue advantage and become scammers and hackers. They are cunning, clever thieves, shrewd statisticians, etc.

3.7 Libra

Librans are those people who always make balance in their relationships. They are looking for harmony, impartiality, and justice with everyone. They always look neat and clean and dislike dirty work of any kind. They are a charming, sensible, modest, gentle, and spendthrift person.

Market place represents these people have the strong business capability. They are diplomatic and interested in their gains but do not like arguments of any kind. They speak the truth and are not interested in making profits by deceiving others. They do not show their anger but create their impact. They are not easily satisfied and being a movable sign, they search here and there for excellence. They like to compromise but don't want to indulge in a fight in any controversial matters. They want to buy peace at any cost and are ready to pay more for that. In any type of quarrel, they prefer not to indulge, keep their mouth close and start avoiding the situation.

Librans are tall and graceful people with a smile on their faces. They are a very social person and very active on social media platforms. They like to comment on social media posts. Being an airy sign of Venus, they are very popular among their friends and pay attention to everyone. They are rarely loners, they have a strong urge for a partner, and therefore, it is very difficult to find any Librans unmarried.

The symbol of the scale of balance represents mental equilibrium and they can see the merits and demerits of an issue. Before concluding, they judge all pros and cons of the situation. Therefore, they are the best judges and good counsellors. A career that involves deciding on taking a review of the situation will bring them success. They can handle tough situations and do not lose their mental balance. But sometimes such quality creates a problem, among too many pros and cons they take much time to take any decision.

Venus ruling of this sign represents a realm of materiality. A positive sign of Venus represents creative qualities like poetic abilities, art, music, dance and drama, philanthropic activities, etc. Venus indicates they are dress-conscious people, like perfumes, properly keeping their documents and files, and live-in beautiful surroundings. They work as musicians, designers, artists, and fashionistas. They are a very hard-working person and want to enjoy all comforts and luxuries of life. They like romantic music and enjoy much in the company of the opposite sex.

Planets in Libra represent that the person is polite in his behaviour, etiquettes and manners are their priorities. They have strong dancing capability and can balance their body swiftly. They are always engaged in doing good deeds and sometimes they take pains to help others. They are the ones who show light to others and listen very carefully to the problems of the other person.

The airy sign represents brilliance and intellect. They are a smart and clever person but not cunning. They are trained and skilled in many arts. They have clear thoughts and can present them in front of others. They like to create an atmosphere of peace and act with consideration. Their decisions are unbiased and they do not favour nepotism.

The opposite side of Libra is Aries which represents that on the top of the mountain person is alone; while Libra - the marketplace, represents the popularity of the person and likes to mingle with others. For Aries 'Spirit' is of great importance but for Libra 'Matter' is prime. The scale represents a balance between the material and spiritual world. A perfectly balanced sign bestows the person luxuries but does not allow them to enjoy.

Affliction: The afflicted sign represents disharmony, unbalanced, perturbed, anxious, tense, and upset nature. It is very difficult for Librans to stay alone. A period of loneliness or isolation is like hell for them. They need motivation in their difficult phase of life. Due to too much consideration, they lack the quality of decisiveness and they need to develop to take prompt decisions. They lack the quality of patience and need to learn to wait.

3.8 Scorpio

Scorpios have inherent probing quality and strong imagination and intuition. Their research capability and investigation power are strong and they like to penetrate secrets but prefer to remain behind the scenes. They have a great understanding of the human mind and a strong capacity to unfold the mystery. To solve the mystery, they collect the information from every nook and corner and absorb every bit of information. They do not trust easily to anyone and like to investigate one thing from various aspects. They become good investigators or detectives and can easily spot hidden things which are difficult and not very obvious to others.

The nature of water is fluid and where it flows it adapts to the nature and shape where it falls. But when it is fixed it becomes murky. When water is stagnant at a place it starts going deep. Therefore, this sign represents deep emotions, underneath the surface and hidden things. Being a fixed watery sign, these natives have strong control of their emotions. This is a sign of transformation; they have great potential to transform themselves and others. A brahmin caste sign represents they work as a healer. Medicine and surgery are also represented by this sign.

They have a strong capability to survive in difficult circumstances. They are persistent and determined to achieve the desired object. They work for long hours and are ready to sacrifice anything for their purpose. Their memory is excellent; they remember everything and never forget even after years. They easily remember all the facts and can bring them to the table when necessary. Their strike is sudden and in arguments, they can surprise the opponents with facts and figures.

Scorpio is the negative sign of Mars. Hence, the malefic nature of Mars; arrogance, autocratic temperament, conflict, chaos, and destruction are also visible here.

They are very stubborn and do not care about criticism. Due to their stubbornness, they don't like a question on their opinion. They can speak for hours and others are there only to listen to them. They believe that they are always right and being a fixed sign, they don't see any reason to change their view. Due to their strong fighting spirit, they never accept defeat and are not ready to compromise under any circumstances. They cannot easily give up and fight for anything which obstructs their desired goal.

Scorpio is the darkest of all the constellations and is related to hidden aspects of life. Therefore, dark, secret and hidden things naturally attract them and they don't want to reveal much about themselves. Scorpio people are so deep that it is very difficult for others to understand them. You can never anticipate the next move of a Scorpio person even after living with them for years. All their actions are in deep silence and they have a great capacity to imbibe all the secrets.

They are extremists, once they have set their goal, they rush to achieve it without wasting a second. They work hard, have intense dedication, and often become workaholics. They are power, position, and money-hungry people. When they are in a power position, they can fire people immediately even the most trusted person without giving any notice.

Scorpio water is muddy water; therefore, for their greed and benefit, they manipulate things. They can manipulate others emotionally as well for their benefit. They say something but deep down they do not follow the same. They keep the important papers underneath the table and wait for even years and take decisions only when the situation turns in their favour and do not bother about others' sufferings.

On the higher aspect, it is the sign of occult, mysticism, secret knowledge, kundalini, and spirituality. The continuous fighting spirit represents till the attainment of "The Ultimate Truth" they will not surrender. The transformation represents low genital pleasure to higher mystical adventure. It is the only sign of the zodiac that has strong potential for both good and evil. With such high energy, the native has the capacity to reach either zenith or nadir depending on their karmas. They best harmonize with Cancer and Pisces.

Affliction: If the sign is afflicted, extreme passion and obsession are also visible. They are rude and cruel in nature and sex-obsessed. They are unreliable and have a connection with illicit people. This sign represents the cunning, revengeful, and relentless nature of a person. Once they are hurt, they do not forgive and take revenge when the time comes and do not bother about repercussions. They can change their decisions at the last minute and do not bother about the harm done to others. They have a controlling attitude towards others and do not like rebellion.

They are highly jealous and possessive and due to this reason sometimes their relationship turns bad. They like to live alone but their craving for a partner is always there who can understand them better. Their nature is stingy and due to the virile Martian energy, they feel pleasure while beating others.

They react very sharply when met with any obstruction from outside. Their hidden and ugly nature is not easily manifested if their feeling is not wounded. It is full of crookedness, vindictiveness, and an acute tendency to hurt not only opponents but also even those whom they like most.

3.9 Sagittarius

This fiery sign indicates enthusiasm, ambition, and aspiration. They are dauntless and confident people; they are not timid and ready to face any situation without any fear. They are wanderers and have a strong desire to increase their knowledge and outlook towards the world.

They are born to explore, and the quest for truth knows no bounds for Sagittarians. They do courageous acts that others hesitate to do. They work on innovative ideas that no one had thought of before and they like to visit new places that others are afraid to go. The more they explore they find that the more exciting world waits for further exploration.

They are philosophical and like to study religious literature and maintain a mini library at home. Like Arjun of Mahabharat, they show their best talent in difficult circumstances. They are not impulsive like Arians and take proper decisions after careful deliberation. They are not in a hurry and delay their plans when they find that planning is not satisfactory. Jupiter is considered an advisor; therefore, they like to advise others. They harmonize best with Arians and Leonians.

Being a Positive and Satwic sign they like only truth. A fierce and fiery sign represents energy, zeal, vigour, passion, and vitality. They fight for justice and being a Kshatriya sign they are ready to pull their sword if they found any injustice is done not only for him but for others also. They are the man of their word and stick with their principles even if the final result would not favourable for them. They speak harsh truth in front of others without any hesitation. Therefore, it is good to discuss any matter in private with Sagittarians.

This dual sign represents a transformation of the person from the beast (half-horse) to the human being (half-man). They become nobler in their life and take interest in spiritual activities. But any transformation is not easy, they have to face various turmoil and challenges in their life. Being a sign of human and animal, their approach is humanitarian. They love to visit forests than a garden and prefer to play outdoor sports over indoor sports.

Due to the fiery sign of Jupiter, they do not like the orders of others. If people politely say so and request them to do so, then they do. They perform better when they have a free hand and no one hinders their decision-making. They are an intuitive person and have good retention power. They are true friends and friendships with Sagittarians last for long years. The 9th house is the house of religion, higher education, and long travel. Planets in the sign represent a person who will take interest in religious activities, higher education, and do long travel in his life.

Affliction: If the sign is afflicted, they lack tact, are not a trustworthy person, and keep false promises. They are fanatics, narrow-minded people, and start the following someone blindly.

3.10 Capricorn

They are very sincere and honest people. Being an earthy sign and ruled by the Saturn, security is the top priority for them and they avoid taking any kind of risk. They check every safety measure before starting the journey and are equipped with every possible equipment that might be needed along the way. They focus only on realistic matters. They don't like to live in dreams and hate to discuss impractical ideas, even if it sounds good to others. In a meeting, they try to remain silent if they are unable to avoid such types of discussions. They are curious and good at planning, practical but stubborn and conservative. They scrutinize the documents very carefully and to investigate any matter, they want to go deep.

Capricorn is the strongest earth sign among the other earthly signs -Taurus and Virgo, which indicates that there are high limits and restrictions. The main idiom of this sign is 'I Utilize' indicates that this sign has a very strong capacity to make full use of available resources. Energy is useful only when it is utilized properly. In this sign, the planet of energy Mars is exalted, which shows that it has a strong power to control and fully utilize energy. Jupiter representing expansion (Aakash-Sky), feels hapless in this sign due to excessive restrictions and is debilitated here.

The planets in this sign indicate that they are very economical and do not like to waste anything. They use all available resources very carefully. They don't like to speculate and invest only in a solid profession after deep scrutiny. They don't shy away from rolling up their sleeves and getting their hands dirty to complete the task and create something incredible. It shows that the person has a strong determination to achieve his goal in life. They have a strong ability to work for long hours without any distractions.

The symbol of the goat represents the sacrificial nature of this sign. The goat has a strong ability to reach the top of the hill amidst various difficulties. Therefore, this symbol represents the ability for an ambitious climb to the top and quiet endurance. They do not trust others and make their way. They are very hardworking and have a strong sense of fulfillment of their duty. They want to enjoy all the luxuries of life and they have a strong ability to work hard to achieve them.

Being a feminine sign and ruled by Saturn, they tend to preserve anything before it goes bad. They are reserved in nature and want to be aloof from others and do not make friends easily. Saturn also represents hindrances, obstacles, and slow movement. The planets in Capricorn indicate that a person has to face all these things in his life but success will come only if he does not leave it.

Affliction: If the sign is afflicted it is very difficult for them to change their conservative thoughts. They are dishonest, miser, greedy, and lethargic. Too much malefic in this sign indicates that the person will not hesitate to commit any crime.

3.11 Aquarius

Aquarians are very social and always try to bring harmony among people but due to the effect of Saturn, they are silent workers. They have their individuality and specialty but due to fixed signs, they do not allow others to enter their circle. Being an airy sign, Aquarians have a great capacity to understand and connect every type of concept and person. Due to fixed sign, they are looking for long-lasting relationships, but they are stubborn and like to stick to their principles.

They have strong patience but they achieve success only after persistent effort. Therefore, they are suitable for research work and for those works where multiple efforts are required. They have a scientific mind and like to research on this line.

Due to the airy sign, they are extremely intelligent and their approach is very practical. They are very idealistic and kindness is in their heart, therefore, they always prefer to support the downtrodden in the society and prefer to work that has humanitarian benefits. They are very sincere and honest and their likes and dislikes are very strong. Being an airy sign, they have a good harmony with the other two airy signs Gemini and Libra.

The quality of the sign is desire (kama); therefore, they have a strong desire for material gain but they are not greedy. They work very hard for what they want but are not willing to take a single pie that is not for their share.

Freedom and independence are the Aquarians' keywords because it is an airy sign and are ruled by Saturn. They prefer friendship and teamwork, but they also need time to be alone for some time to rejuvenate themselves. Because it is a fixed sign, they have strong opinions and don't go back down from an argument. They have a strong ability to see both sides of a coin which makes them excellent problem-solvers. Planets in this sign, show that the person prefers their individuality and doesn't like to interfere with any person.

Due to the element of air and relation with water they are deep thinkers and have strong retention power. With their penetrating eyes, they can read the hidden motives of others and they hate flattery and hypocrisy. They are very adaptable to the situation and capable of conquering boundaries.

Co-rulership of Uranus represents; occult, radical changes, revolution, innovation, technology, and surprising events. It is a fixed sign ruled by Saturn, so they are very lazy people and do not move from their place even after shouting a lot. On the positive side, they have a strong ability to sit in a place for long periods of time, have strong powers of concentration and can become true seekers of truth who sit in deep meditation at one place.

Affliction: Sometimes it seems that everything is in their head on the other hand sometimes they are very moody, eccentric, rebellious, and unconventional. The afflicted air element in this sign results in disharmony or break up in a long relationship.

3.12 Pisces

Pisces is ruled by Jupiter which represents philosophy, knowledge, and wisdom. Under the influence of Jupiter, Pisces people are honest people and try to avoid any kind of conflict. They are not combative and do not like to participate in cut-throat competitions. They act as a mediator among many tussles. Due to a feminine sign, they are a very modest person and always behave in a very polite manner. Due to their truthiness, they easily believe in their friends but later regret, because they forget that there are not only true human beings but also evil ones present in this world and it is not always good to trust everyone.

They never leave any work in the middle and try to complete it before taking on any new task. They have a sharp memory and being a watery sign, they adapt to any kind of situation. They are kind and are very loyal people. They are also very moody persons and if Moon is afflicted in a person's birth chart, the native is always in dilemma and never takes any decision on time.

They tend to forgive their enemies but when they are angry, they easily withdraw their shield of help from others. The exaltation of Venus here indicates that they are very good at advisory services. The feminine qualities of receptivity, sense of security, and parenting are visible here. They are very sensitive people and can capture the hidden thoughts and feelings of others.

The key phrase – 'I believe' shows they tend to have beliefs on their feelings and intuitions. Among three watery signs Cancer, Scorpio and Pisces; Pisces water is ocean water which represents depth in their personality. They are cold and wet, and in the winter season, they feel very cold compared to other people. In western astrology, Pisces is co-ruled by the planet Neptune (God of the Ocean) which represents idealists, imagination, illusion, escapism, and mysticism.

On the higher side, it represents visionaries, glamorous and charismatic personalities. For Pisceans dreams, myths and fantasies feel more real than ordinary life. Like a fish in an ocean, they are a very creative and movable person but feel like a fish out of water when their creativity is not used.

This 12th sign is the last sign of the zodiac, the journey that started from Aries is going to end here now, this is the sign of salvation. Therefore, they have a strong desire for spirituality and want to study astrology and other occult sciences. A strong sign produces great artists and creative personalities and some time in life they delve into the ocean of spiritualism.

Affliction: On a day of thick fog over the sea, it is difficult to look ahead and differentiate between the sea and the sky. That shows illusionary, day-dreamers, and away from reality, if this sign is afflicted. To escape their boring mundane life, they may indulge in alcohol and drugs or indulge in other wrong ways to forget their misery. They are slow to react and have a dull personality.

Chapter 4

Profession & Related Houses

The twelve houses of astrology represent different areas of life. Out of these, the eleventh house represents income or gains. Without income, no one can survive in this world. In modern times, it is represented by paper currency but since ancient times, it has been represented by gold. The economy is based on gold and paper currency is backed by gold reserves. So, income means gold and efforts must be made to generate income and it should not be haphazard. When the effort is done systematically it is called a skill. Learning is necessary to become skilled and childhood is the age when a person learns faster because children are flexible. ***In other words, learning new skills requires childlike flexibility.***

Jupiter represents gold and the higher aspect of Jupiter is Lord Vishnu running the whole universe. Gold (Money) is important for movement as it opens up opportunities for what you want to do. But the purpose of life is not the collection of gold, Jupiter represents the sky. Money is a fickle thing, it comes and goes as no one keeps the sky in a box. As the money starts increasing, man's expansion starts increasing and ego starts growing. Therefore, after Jupiter in the solar system, there is Saturn which eliminates every excess done by Jupiter.

Mercury is considered a child and it represents our learning ability. Without any skill, no person can earn, so a strong Mercury is required to become a highly skilled person.

For earnings, whether from a job or business, the power of two planets is important – Mercury and Jupiter. For service, the strength of the sixth house, and for business the strength of seventh house is important in both D1 and D10 charts. The 10th house and the placement of its lord in D1 and D10 chart is important for success in either business or service. Before arriving at any conclusion, one should also consider the time, situation and place where the native is living and the results should not be taken verbatim.

For career success in any field, it should be kept in mind that there should be a good relationship between the lord of the lagna in D1 chart and the lord of the lagna in D10 chart. For example, suppose the lord of the lagna in the D1 chart is the Sun and the lord of the lagna in the D10 chart is Jupiter, both these planets have a good relationship with each other, then the career of the person flourishes as both the lords support each other. But if Saturn is the lord of the lagna instead of Jupiter in D10 then such a person has to face many struggles to succeed in his career.

4.1 Houses for Success in Service

For service, it is important to see the strength of the sixth house in both D1 and D10 horoscopes. If the sixth house is stronger than the seventh house, then the person will go for service. The sixth house is related to daily activities and the planets in this house indicates that the person is happy with his routine. He goes to his job every morning and returns home every evening and his routine is the same every day.

It is related to our digestive system and when there is a disturbance in it, the person becomes ill, so the sixth house is also called the “house of illness”. A weak house indicates weak immunity also problem related to service. When a person is sick, he cannot go to work and his income is affected. Therefore, for success in service, the sixth house needs to be strong.

4.2 Houses for Success in Business

For business, it is necessary to observe the strength of the 7th house in both D1 and D10 charts. Because in business a person has to deal with many people and enter into various agreements and partnerships. The house of partnerships (7th) should be stronger than the house of daily activities (6th), otherwise, the person may fail in his venture. We should also consider the following points.

i. Ascendant (Lagna) - Check the total number of Lagna in the Ashtakvarga table. It should be more than 28. Check the planets in Lagna and the position of Lagna lord in D1, D9 and D10 chart. Lagna indicates the general nature of a person and his prominent traits. A weak lagna affected by malefic planets shows that the person is timid, unable to walk alone, and always looking for support.

ii. The 2nd House: This is the house of savings, property and resources. To save money, the second house needs to be strong. Earth signs indicate availability of resources, so earth signs in the second house indicate wealth. The placement of 2nd lord indicates utilization of resources and way of savings. Check the triangle of 2nd, 6th and 10th house in D9 chart. These are earth houses and planets and signs here indicate the way of wealth and savings. For example, if the second house in D9 chart is Scorpio then such a person will use hidden activities to collect money and if the malefic planets are placed then he will use illegal means to save. But if the second house is Sagittarius then the person cannot do any wrong thing for money.

iii. The 3rd House: This is the house of courage and Mars is the significator of this house. Courage is needed to move ahead on an unknown path. Where nothing is clear, the energy of Mars is ready to accept the challenge and step on the unknown path. If the decision goes wrong, the person is ready to bear the pain, but this energy does not let him sit quietly. When everything is decided, then it is routine and there is no point in showing courage there.

Therefore, check the position of Mars, its aspect or Pativartana Yoga related to the third house. A strong third house is required for any endeavor and the position of its lord shows the connection with the steps taken by the person.

iv. The 5th House: This is the house of creativity and self-expression. Planets in the 5th house indicates creativity, inclination and the position of 5th lord indicates that the person like to engage himself in that type of activities. Every business carries some risk, therefore, a strong 5th house is necessary to access the risk and take timely action.

The fire sign in the 5th house represents a person of action. They are in the spotlight because of their work and are able to walk alone. The earth sign represents money and strategic action; the air sign represents networking and fame; the water sign represents empathy, compassion, and nurturing qualities. Each element has different characteristics, so it is important to observe the natural inclinations of the person. The person takes interest in the element associated with the 5th house and the placement of its lord.

This is the house of speculation and Rahu is the planet for speculation and gambling. The influence of Rahu indicates that the person will take an interest in these activities.

v. The 7th House: From the 1st house to the 6th house represents our individuality, till here the soul is individual, but now it is in search of a partner which is represented by the seventh house. Business means dealing with other persons, therefore, the 7th house must be strong, and benefic planets indicate smooth progress. It is the most important house for business and without a strong 7th house a person may fail in his endeavor.

The seventh house is also the house of war, in case of conflict, a fight starts with the partner and the matter goes to court. Whether the matter is between two countries or individuals, the war always begins from the seventh house. The word partnership is not limited to sharing the profits from business but it has a wider meaning. Partnership flourishes only when the person respects his partner. Every customer or client is a partner in a business because you are building a relationship with them. But when a businessman starts being dishonest and unfaithful, then conflict begins.

A person enters into marriage because he needs a partner and does not want to be alone. He is looking for happiness and wants to make his life better. Similarly, every item brought by a person to his home creates a partnership with its provider. Every item we bring to our home has the sole purpose that it will help us make our lives better. The seventh house relates to all those things we form relationships with.

For example, we buy a consumer goods or avail a service with the intention that it will help us improve our lives and we develop a relationship with its provider. What if the goods or service provider delivers poor quality items? Then a dispute arises between the two parties and the matter goes to court.

In earlier times, people used to bring in the army to settle disputes and decide the matter by fighting, but now time have been changed, and the matter goes to court. But the issue is still the same that one party cheated the other party. The seventh house is the house of business contracts and agreements and when one party breaks the contract, conflict starts between the two. So, the seventh house is for both business and conflict (war).

In the natural zodiac, Libra is in the 7th house that represents the market. Deals are made in the market, when the fork of the scale stops at the balance point then both parties agree to the deal. So, balance is most important in business, and those who can bring balance and avoid conflict are the ones who are successful in business. A successful businessman always respects his partners, respects his customers, and always tries to avoid conflict.

vi. The 8th House: This is the house of sudden changes, unforeseen events, transformation, insurance, unexpected financial gains and losses. Loans are important for business and it requires both short-term and long-term loans. According to Phaladeepika the 6th house is related to debt (ch-1, sh-13). Benefic 6th and 8th houses indicate that the person will get loans easily. The 6th house indicates taking a loan, the 8th house indicates possession and utilization of money because it is 2nd to the 7th house, and the 12th house indicates its repayment as repaying a loan is an expense for the native. Benefics in the 8th house indicate proper utilization of the loan. In contrast, malefic indicates problems related to debt and money loss because the 7th house represents with whom the transaction has taken place. Therefore, careful observation of the 6th, 8th and 12th houses is necessary for debt-related matters.

The 8th house is the house of retirement. When it is active the person leads a life of retirement or does work related to retirement. It also indicates that the person will engage in some activity whose fruits will be visible to the person at the age of retirement. Retirement means a continuous flow of income without any hard work as the person has already sown the seeds and now he is enjoying the fruits. Strong planets in the 8th house signify inheritance, legacy and windfall gains. This is the house where all secret things reside and get revealed in an unexpected manner. A poorly placed and weak house indicates debt-related problems.

Mars is the planet of debt and loans. If Mars is positive then the native gets loans easily and uses it for growth, while negative Mars indicates that there may be financial instability due to increasing debt. Despite earning sufficient income, a person remains in debt.

Jupiter indicates expansion, it also indicates that one can get loans easily but too much debt creates repayment problems. For business related loans it is necessary to check the strength of the 8th house in D10 chart. It is related with loans, retirement, and insurance. Check the relationship of Mars with the 8th house in D10 chart, such a person can get loans easily and works as a debt, insurance and retirement consultant.

vii. The 9th House: This house is related to international affairs. If the 9th house of a person is strong then he can enter the international markets. Find the connection between the 5th house and the 9th house, the creativity, talent, ideas, and thoughts of such a person spread in the international market. The 9th house represents luck, auspicious planets support the luck of the person.

In the natural zodiac, Sagittarius sign represents the 9th house. Hence, planets placed in Sagittarius sign play a vital role in entering the international markets.

viii. The 10th House: This is explained in detail in Chapter 8.

ix. The 11th House: It is the second house from the 10th house and is associated with gains from work. It is the house of our hopes, desires and aspirations. The 11th house considers our group and collective activities.

In the natural zodiac, Aquarius sign represents the 11th house. It is associated with our contribution to the betterment of humanity and society. Planets in the 11th house indicates teamwork and relation with the friends.

4.3 Active Houses

It is important to know which house is currently active in the horoscope. Without knowing the active house, man's efforts do not give proper results because every house has its time to get active and the current Mahadasha-Antardasha and transiting planets influence it. Following are the steps to know which house is currently active;

i. Check the current Mahadasha and Antardasha. Tick the planets and their respective houses in the horoscope.

ii. Check the planets and their signs in transit in the horoscope. Tick their placement-aspect-conjunction.

iii. The houses which have more than two ticks are active houses as long as the dasha and transit are present.

Example:

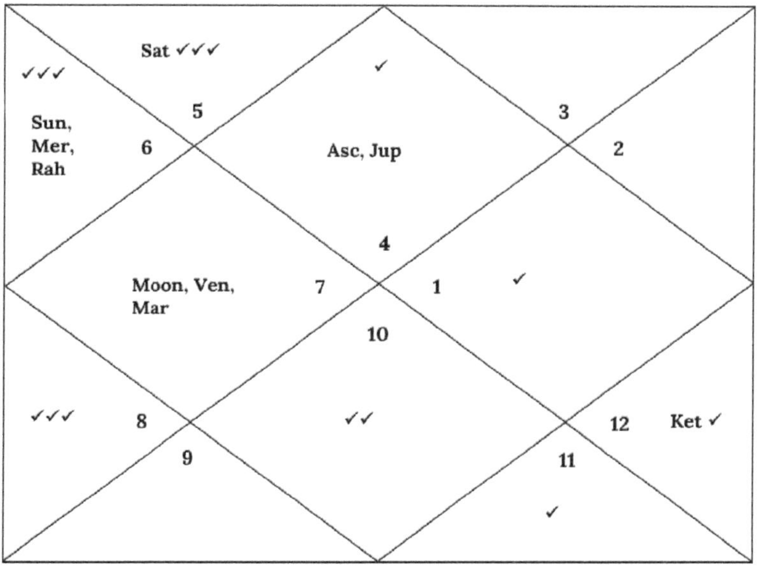

Mahadasha and Antardasha Analysis

i. The current Mahadasha and Antardasha of the native is of Saturn-Sun. So, currently Saturn and Sun are active in their horoscope.

ii. Saturn is the Lord of Capricorn and Aquarius and in the above horoscope, it is placed in the 2nd house. So, tick the 2nd house and 7th and 8th house.

iii. Sun is the Lord of Leo and is placed in the 3rd house. So, tick the 2nd house and 3rd house.

Transit Analysis of Saturn, Jupiter and Rahu - Ketu

i. Currently, Saturn is in Aquarius in transit and in the horoscope, it is the 8th house. But there is no planet in the 8th house, so we do not put another tick there, because there is no conjunction there.

ii. Saturn has three aspects - 3rd, 7th and 10th. From the 8th house its 3rd aspect is on 10th house, 7th aspect is on the 3rd house and 10th aspect is on the 5th house. We will tick all these houses.

iii. Jupiter is in Taurus in transit and in the horoscope, it is the 11th house. But there is no planet in the 11th house, so we do not put a tick there, because there is no conjunction there.

iv. Jupiter has three aspects – 5th, 7th and 9th. From 11th house its 5th aspect is on the 3rd house, 7th aspect is on the 5th house and 9th aspect is on the 7th house. We will tick all these houses.

v. Currently, Rahu is transiting in Pisces and it is the 9th house in the horoscope. Ketu is placed in the 9th house and Rahu is transiting over it. Ketu represents the headless body and Rahu is the head. So, in the transit, the body has got the head and when both are joined the body is complete, you can do whatever you think. The same phenomenon is happening in the 3rd house where Rahu is placed. The head has got its body. So, Rahu transiting over Ketu and Ketu transiting over Rahu play an important role in life because whatever the person was thinking of doing for a long time, he can do it now. So, we will tick to the 3rd house and the 9th house.

vi. Rahu has three aspects – 5th, 7th and 9th, while Ketu has no aspects. From 9th house its 5th aspect is on ascendant, 7th aspect is on the third house and 9th aspect in on the 5th house. We will tick all these houses.

Analysis: When we count all the ticks, we can see that the 2nd house, the 3rd house and the 5th house has got three ticks. The 7th house has two ticks and the 8th, 9th, 10th and ascendant has only one tick. Now, we categorize the level of activity in three levels - Highly active, moderately active, and low active.

i. Highly Active – Those houses that have two or more ticks and the house lord is active can be considered highly active houses. So, currently, the 2nd and the 7th houses are highly active house in this horoscope.

ii. Moderately active - Those houses that have two or more ticks but the house lord is not active, we can consider them moderately active houses. So, the 3rd and the 5th house are moderately active houses.

iii. Low Active - Those houses only have one tick we can consider as a low active house. So, currently the 7th, 8th, 9th, 10th, and ascendant are low active houses.

The above analysis indicates that efforts should be made in those houses which are highly active because they are getting more energy. Energy needs direction and by channelizing it in the right direction we can achieve success in our efforts. Also, we can know which house is going to be active in the coming time and we can make proper preparations for it in advance.

Chapter 5

Planets & Profession

Vedic astrology believes in the influence of nine planets in our birth chart. The characteristics of these planets affect the profession of a person. The planets situated in a house and their transit generate a specific energy and that energy affects the person concerned and all the circumstances related to him.

Selection of a career in today's world is very important, people wander here and there to find a suitable career. Information about the ruling planet of profession can help a lot to find the natural inclination of the person. The 2nd, 6th and 10th houses are earthy signs which represents materialism and their lord play an important role in career selection. There is a relation between our savings (2nd house), our day-to-day life (6th house), and our karma (10th house). Hence, the triangle of earthy houses and the placement of their lord is necessary to observe in D1 and D9 chart.

Moon rules our mind, hence the position of the Moon and the 10th house from the Moon is also important to consider. Navamsha chart is necessary to analyze and the position of 10th lord of D1 chart in Navamsha is taken into consideration. The planet which is more powerful among them determines the career of the native.

5.1 The Sun

The Sun is called the king of all planets and is the source of all existence in our solar system. The shining Sun in the sky represents strength, energy, and vitality. It represents the power of resistance. It is bold and forceful. It represents mental strength and confidence. It represents our ego and pride. It represents father, authority, government, and honor from government, high status, fame, victory, and enlightenment. Strong Sun in the horoscope makes a person determined and decisive. It gives high energy, commanding power, quality of leadership, respect of elders, and good quality of listening.

A strong Sun represents a charismatic personality. The person will be ambitious, energetic, influential, and kind-hearted. The person will be courageous enough to go alone, even in difficult circumstances without any fear. He will not be ready to compromise anything for his dignity and honor. In my corporate career, I have seen that people are ready to quit their jobs but are not ready to compromise on their dignity if the Sun is strong on their chart. They are ready to bear anything in life for their self-respect. In such a situation, worshiping the Sun God daily is beneficial for the person.

Sun gets exalted in Aries, a fiery sign of Mars. Aries represents the solo spirit and does not wait for others to come. Aries means – at the top of the mountain alone. The nature of this sign is suitable for the Sun – King, so, it is exalted here. While Libra is a marketplace, is totally against the tendency of the Sun. Therefore, the Sun gets debilitated in Libra.

Sun controls our eyesight, to regain eye-sight and vitality in life people in India worship Lord Sun. When the sunlight comes everything is visible. In the same way, wherever the Sun is placed in your chart everything will become visible and you cannot hide it.

Sun Represents:

1. Gold, copper, ruby, spectacles, jewellery, medicines and its related business.

2. In association with Jupiter it rules banking and financial institution. In association with Mars it rules electrical and electronic goods and all business related to it.

3. Government, government services and their departments. Heads of corporations, influential political leaders, ministers, senior officials with decision-making power.

4. It represents places of worship and temples, mountain trees, and pungent taste like; onion, ginger, black pepper, chilies, etc.

5. It represents coarse clothes, Kshatriya (warrior) caste and the age of 50 years old.

6. It represents red color, summer season and organic matter.

7. It represents bones, average height, steadfast tendency, and upward direction.

Profession: A strong Sun is important to work with the government, get a high-ranking government service and to become an influential political leader. It indicates success in subjects and professions related to Physics, Statistics, Mathematics, Political Science, Astronomy, Ayurveda, Medicine, Electricity, Business given by father, Bureaucrats, Administrative jobs, Presidents, Politicians, CEOs, Magistrates, Rulers, Jewelers, Goldsmith, Financier, etc.

Affliction: An afflicted Sun indicates that the person will easily become tempered. Such a person is arrogant, jealous, irritable, dominating, pretentious, lavish, conceit, and haughty. Such people do not listen to anyone and consider themselves supreme. Sun is a fiery planet which creates isolation. Sun represents ego, ego creates heat and heat creates isolation. Such a person has to live a lonely life and people becomes afraid to go to near to him.

5.2 The Moon

Moon is a Sattvic planet and controls our minds. It is a feminine planet, represents mother in the chart, peace of mind, and rules our emotions. It represents selflessness like a mother and the tender qualities of a female. It represents the nourishing quality, sensitivity, and imagination of the person. A strong Moon indicates a strong mind, friendly nature, and pleasing personality. The person is receptive, decisive, mature, helpful in nature, and clear in his thoughts. Such a person never wastes time in vain things, wants the discussion to come to the point, and takes no interest in idle gossip. Being the representative of the mother in the horoscope, the person should always respect his mother and should never quarrel with her, if he wants that his Moon always remains strong.

The fourth house is the house of public and the Moon rules the public. If the Moon is placed in the fourth house, it gets directional strength and the native gets its positive qualities. Moon being a feminine planet bestows attractiveness and other feminine qualities. The person under the influence of the Moon as a ruling planet takes interest in taking care of others.

It indicates professions related to fluids, doctors, psychologists, therapists, child care, and other nurturing and healing professions. Following are a few qualities of the Sun and the Moon;

1. The Sun represents the father, the Moon represents the mother.

2. The Sun represents the seed, the Moon represents the womb.

3. The Sun represents the order and the Moon represents the fulfillment of the order.

4. Sun is the source of light and the moon has no light and always depends on sunlight. Sun represents a person's active nature and moon represents his passive nature.

5. The Sun shows independence and the weak Moon indicates that the person is looking for support and is always afraid of being alone.

6. The Sun represents the present, the Moon represents the past.

7. If Moon is situated in any house from the 9th to 12th house, then the person takes interest in subjects like; History, Archaeology, Astrology, etc. The person memorizes the dates of historical events easily and is quick to learn these subjects.

When the Moon placed less than 72 degrees from the Sun, it indicates less sunlight and due to absence of sunlight the native is prone to diseases easily. Such native must worship lord Sun in his whole life.

The sign of Taurus is highly suitable for the Moon. Taurus is a feminine sign - fertile and receptive, it is a highly fertile land in the zodiac. The nature of Taurus is to produce and grow things. Its symbol is the bull which is known for its sensuality and fertility. Taurus represents luxury and comfort, therefore, the Moon - the Queen, finds this sign perfectly suitable for herself, and becomes exalted at 3 degrees in the sign (Upon entering here, the queen found a very suitable place for her stay). Scorpio is a sign of ruthlessness and represents muddy water which is totally against the nature of the Moon - the Queen, and it gets debilitated in the sign while entering (3 degrees).

Moon Represents:

1. Moon is a watery planet, represents moist and rainy season and watery places like; well, water tanks, bathrooms, watery surfaces, rivers, bays, ocean, etc.

2. It represents white things and short height.

3. It represents new fabric and organic matter.

4. It represents salty taste (sea salt, rock salt), gems, spotless pearls, silver, and other white metals.

5. It belongs to the Vaishya (Merchant) caste and represents the age of 70 years old.

6. It represents the coconut tree, fruits, vegetables, and all watery substances.

7. It represents aluminium products, boat clubs, swimming pools.

8. It represents snow, powdered products, marine products, conch, stout sugarcane, water tanks, fishing and fish industry.

Profession: The Moon indicates profession related to the Shipping industry, Navy, Water department, Milk and other liquids, Jobs related to fruits and vegetables, Nurturing and helping jobs, Tour & Travel, Air hostess, Liquor, Cloth, Herbs, Caterers, Chemicals, Medical field, Para-Medical staff, Laundry, Fine arts, Music, Dance, Pharmacy, Bio-Chemistry, Environmental sciences, Agriculture, Navy, Journalism, Advertising, Hospitals, Plants, Nursery, Marine, Sailor, etc.

Affliction: An afflicted moon indicates a person will become depressed, pessimistic, impulsive, timid and over-anxious, dreamers, self-destructive, insane, and psychic. A weak moon indicates a person can be easily influenced by outside energies and unable to take decisive decisions.

5.3 Mars

Mars is considered a Tamasic and fiery planet. It is a malefic and ruthless planet. Being the lord of weapons and war, Mars does not think twice before taking the initiative. If it is favorable in the horoscope, it bestows good qualities. One will be courageous, will fight evils, and will do heroic deeds. The character of a person is strong, determined, passionate and the person is not afraid of any kind of obstacles in life. He is a great protector and always uses his sword to protect others. He can go to any extent to save someone's life.

Mars represents the drive, courage, initiation, and adventurous nature of the person. It represents determination, confidence, sharp wit, and leadership quality. The position of Mars in the birth chart shows where the physical activity will take place and indicates what kind of things will excite you, how you deal with disputes and react to stressful situations, violence, etc. Mars represents the younger brother, land, and property and rules the animal instincts in man. Mars believes in overcoming obstacles by force rather than any strategy. This indicates the impulsive nature of a person with a quick activity.

Martians are the pioneers and have risk-taking inclinations. It belongs to entrepreneurs, conquerors, adventurers, and athletes. They like to conduct large-scale operations that requires high energy. Mars indicates new ventures and its beneficial aspects indicate the floating of new companies.

As Commander-in-Chief, the most important thing for Mars is to win the battle. Similarly, the most important thing for a quarrelsome person is to win the argument, no matter how. Therefore, a wise man never indulges in any discussion with such a person. An afflicted Mars indicates that the person can go to any extreme to win the argument and fight.

Mars represents action and energy. Action without a goal is a waste of energy. The energy of Mars should be used in a constructive manner and in spiritual activities. Mars gets exalted in Capricorn, a sign of Saturn. Capricorn represents a high level of restrictions and control. In this sign, Martian energy is fully controlled; when energy is fully controlled it produces maximum results. Mars gets exalted at 28 degrees in Capricorn, at this point, Mars energy is fully controlled (However, Saturn treats Mars as its enemy). Cancer, a sign of the Moon has no power to control Martian energy. Therefore, Mars gets debilitated in this sign.

We move into this world due to Martian energy. To burn energy, fuel is required and that fuel is our desire. If the fuel (desire) produces smoke, it not only disturbs the life of the person but also the environment around him. Mars represents fire, and the scar of fire does not go easily. Therefore, one must control Martian energy in a constructive manner so that it should not produce smoke and should not leave a scar.

Mars indicates physical sports and exercise, the iron and steel industry, police department, firefighting department, military activities, etc. It represents fiery places like; the kitchen, engine room, and boilers. It indicates cuts, wounds, scars, strikes, conspiracy, criminals, murderers, thieves, robbers, etc.

Mars Represents:

1. It is a masculine, kshatriya (warrior) caste planet and represents upward movement.

2. It is a dry and barren planet and indicates a tense and quarrelsome situation.

3. It represents accidents, fires, disputes, destruction, wars, and sexual drive.

4. Its color is blood-red and stone coral.

5. It represents the summer season and fiery places.

6. It deals with burnt clothing and inorganic substances.

7. It represents young age and low height.

8. Its taste is bitter and the tendency is violent.

9. It represents iron & steel, electricity, furnace, tobacco, cigarette, cement (with Saturn), stones, marbles, bombs and explosives.

Profession: Mars indicates weapons of all kinds and is considered the lord of war. It indicates any job related to these fields like; Military and police departments. Any type of job involving small or large metal tools such as; Dentist, Engineering job, Hunter, Butcher, Barber, etc. Mars gives success in subjects and professions related to; Metals, Surgeons, Arms and ammunitions, Explosives, Fireworks, Furnaces, Athletes, Butchers, Gyms, Wrestling, Mechanics, Cooks, Blacksmiths, Property, Geology, Adventurous sports, etc.

Affliction: If the planet is afflicted then the person will use all his power to fulfil his desire and can go to any extent. Irrespective of how many fingers are burnt, the fulfilment of desire is very important for him and if the person is running on the Mahadasha of Mars, then dangerous consequences can be possible, as he is not ready to give up his desire under any circumstances. A weak and afflicted Mars makes the native a sexual pervert.

The afflicted Mars indicates that the native will easily lose his temper and start abusing others without thinking. The person will become quarrelsome and will be ready to fight over trivial matters; Scratches on a car and people are ready to fight on the street. The afflicted Mars does not like differences of opinion with anyone. The native will argue in vain, instead of giving any intelligent argument, he prefers to use force and feels the joy of winning the battle.

5.4 Mercury

Mercury is a Rajasic planet, it is considered a child and children have a tendency to imitate elders. Similarly, Mercury reflects the characteristics of the planet with which it is associated. Children must be nurtured by their parents and elders. Similarly, Mercury must be associated with benefics. Mercury alone in a house or its association with malefics does not produce good results.

Mercury indicates how we express ourselves to the outside world. It indicates literary pursuit and makes a person good at speaking, learning, proficient in many languages, and orator. It represents analytical ability, planning, diplomacy, accounting, ideas, thoughts, talkative person, jokes, intelligence, writing, editing, publishing, etc. It indicates colleges, schools, shops, and market place.

Mercury creates a sharp mind, awareness, deep research, and mystery seekers. Strong mercury is required to be good at math and astrology. It indicates that the person will be able to grasp the subject quickly, have good retentive power, and will be strong in mental calculations. Mercury indicates connections, many friends, correspondence, news, and information. Mercury is mutable and represents restlessness and lack of consistency. Therefore, Mercurians must learn stability and perseverance in their lives.

The position of Mercury in the horoscope shows a curious person. It shows the agility, simplicity, and versatile nature of the person. However, if the person keeps a firm and stable attitude and leaves his restless nature then he will perform better in his work. Mercury being a mutable planet indicates that if a person keeps himself too busy in work, he will leave it after some time. So, people who are too obsessed about work and forget day and night, one day they leave it from their life forever. A day comes when they do not want to discuss it. Excessive involvement leads to separation.

This is how the principle of excessive busyness works. This is how Mercury's fickle energy works until a person's curiosity turns into his thirst for knowledge. Intelligence is like a double-edged sword, so Mercury must be conjunct or aspected by auspicious planets.

Mercury's exaltation sign is Virgo – a Mooltrikona sign of Mercury. The sign of Virgo represents virginity and celibacy. Mercury is considered an adolescent as it is yet to attain maturity. Mercury exalted in Virgo indicates that a teenager should follow the path of celibacy to make his mind sharp. Pisces represents sexual pleasure, if a teenager indulges in sexual activities, his Mercury will be debilitated and he will lose courage and ability to speak when needed. Indulgence in sexual activity will also hamper the development of his mind. Such a person will not get a sharp mind in his life; he will remain a person of a very mediocre mind and will never be able to become an intelligent and wise person.

Mercury Represents:

1. Its color is green, and the stone is emerald.

2. It represents playgrounds, living beings and wet clothes.

3. Its metal is alloy and gender is eunuch.

4. It belongs to the Vaishya (Merchant) caste and represents trading activities.

5. It represents mixed tastes and a mixture of diverse qualities. A strong mercury indicates versatility.

6. It represents skin, short in height, and sideways momentum.

7. It represents wet crop, brinjal, ladyfinger, beetroot, etc.

8. It belongs to the Sharad season (from 20 Sept. to 19 Nov. approx.).

Profession: Accounts, Commerce, Insurance, Investments, Banks, Money, Publishing, Books, Journalism, Treasury, Telecommunication, Transportation, Trading, Broking, Astrology, Chartered Accountants, Journalism, Writer, Publisher, Teacher, Mathematics, Media, Web designing, Secretary, Clerk, Broker, Public relations, Messenger, Interpreter, Procession related to communication of any kind, Diplomats, Negotiators, Courier Services, Stenographer, Booksellers, Architect, Reporter, Merchandise, etc.

Affliction: Afflicted mercury indicates native will be cunning, liar, eccentric, scandalous, cheater, argumentative, unprincipled, and boastful. It shows the person may be gullible or will cheat his clients and run away with their money. Poor mercury indicates lack of concentration, changing moods, and poor memory.

Afflicted Mercury Creates Jealously: Children pretend to be in pain to avoid going to school. They are jealous of other children and lie to escape punishment. Children are innocent and try their best to make people believe them. Similarly, an afflicted Mercury shows that such a person does not hesitate to lie for his selfishness. An afflicted Mercury gives rise to jealousy and such people become jealous of the success of their friends or close ones and try to harm them secretly. This is similar to the behavior of a child who is jealous of something that another child has and he does not have. For example, when a person buys a car and his neighbor does not have one, then out of jealousy he secretly scratches the car and when asked he acts innocent like a child.

When people are jealous they try to hide their true feelings but negativity builds up in their mind. They behave innocently like children but this jealousy forces them to do something negative if Mercury is influenced by malefic planets. If Mercury is influenced by Rahu then such people hide their identity and post wrong comments on social media or make insulting comments jokingly.

Due to this negativity, an immature person unwilling to accept the success of his friends and colleagues. When caught they behave like children, pretend to be innocent, change their statements, and try to escape punishment. They try their best to convince people that they are right and this behavior is exactly like that of a child. A mature person never envies others. In fact, he claps when his friends and colleagues achieve success through their hard work.

5.5 Jupiter

Jupiter is considered to be the master. It represents the generosity of the person. Being Dev Guru, one should always respect Jupiter. In the same manner, the person having strong Jupiter attracts respect from others. Jupiter is considered a counsellor and represents all counselling activities. Jupiter provides wisdom and removes ignorance and darkness. A strong Jupiter indicates a very honest person. He is dutiful and respects law and religion. He is a magnanimous and broad-minded person and does not believe in any type of fighting and works on making the atmosphere congenial. He believes in co-operation, works on a strategy, and waits for the outcome patiently.

Jupiter provides education, interest in religion, spiritual rhymes, philosophy, astrology, and law. A strong Jupiter indicates concentration, mediation, reading habits, thrust for knowledge, benevolence, prudent behaviour, ethics, morals, etc. Jupiter represents abundance, when it is favourable; opportunity knocks on your door. A person having strong Jupiter in his chart never breaches anyone's trust. The person will always show respect to others, favour doing the right things, and follow the path of justice. By the grace of Jupiter, a person becomes wise, knowledgeable in scriptures and gets expertise in one or more subjects. Knowledge does not come without a price, so no one gives importance to free advice.

Jupiter always prevents the native from difficulties as long as the native follow the righteous path in his life. The person will be protected at the last moment in a state of difficulty when every possible hope is over. Like a guru teaches lessons to his students and provides his guidance and protection as long as the student follows the guru's advice, but when the student stops listening to the guru after several warnings, the guru simply removes his protective shield. This is the way Jupiter works.

Jupiter punishes the person but not like Mars. Mars's attack is direct and sharp but Jupiter simply goes away without saying anything. When Jupiter becomes malefic, he removes his shield and stops giving direction. Without direction, the person wanders here and there and wastes his time and energy. Due to the absence of Jupiter, the direction fades away from the person's life and his futile wandering starts without any result. The darkness of ignorance gradually submerges the person.

Jupiter represents growth, and the freshwater of Cancer represents life as well as growth. Therefore, Jupiter feels most comfortable in the sign of Cancer and gets exalted here. Cancer is the fourth sign of the zodiac which is ruled by the Moon. The fourth house also represents the mother's womb. A pregnant woman is the best example of Jupiter exalted in Cancer. The unborn baby (fetus) growing in the womb floats in the fluid, indicating life expands in the water.

Swami Vivekananda said, "Strength is Life, Weakness is Death. Expansion is Life, Contraction is Death. Love is Life, Hatred is Death". Jupiter represents all the positive qualities said in the quote.

Jupiter represents a person who fulfils his promises and never breaches anyone's trust if a person does against this then Jupiter removes its shield of protection. Jupiter gets debilitated in Capricorn; a sign ruled by Saturn.

Capricorn is a sign of a high level of control, restrictions, and limitations. A planet of expansion – Jupiter, feels completely hapless in this sign. A debilitated Jupiter in a chart indicates that a person wants to do various things in his life, but has to face a problem of lack of resources. He will complete the task only by moving inch by inch.

Jupiter rules our big plans and bestows us, children. When a couple has a child, various necessities of the child start and they take interest in the fulfillment of all these activities, representing the expansion of life in this mundane world. Children are our future; therefore, Jupiter represents the future.

Jupiter is our luck; therefore, people say when someone is going to do an act when the outcome is unknown "Best of Luck", seeking blessings of Lord Jupiter. Jupiter represents the person who follows principles and does not deviate from the chosen path. Materialistic desire does not allure the person, he prefers to face any situation in life but does not ready to surrender his respect.

Jupiter represents; schools and colleges, law-court, temples, places of sermons, legislative assembly, charitable institutions, bank buildings, hospitals, asylums, and all fatty and sweet products. Jupiter represents the husband in the female horoscope. If a native is running from Jupiter Mahadasha or in transit affected by Jupiter, the native has the inclination to eat more sweets than his normal eating.

Physicians write “Rx” at the top of the prescription before writing their medical advice and seek the blessings of Jupiter. Rx is the Latin symbol for the planet Jupiter. Medical astrology states that taking medicine in Jupiter Hora is more beneficial than at any other time.

In which house Jupiter is situated represents an expansion on matters related to the house. Jupiter’s placement in a chart indicates a person will adopt ethical principles and take interest in the expansion of activities related to the house concerned. It also indicates that our luck resides there.

Jupiter Represents:

1. It is a watery and sattvic planet.

2. It is a masculine, brahmin (scholar) caste planet and represents ether.

3. Its color is yellow, the stone is yellow sapphire, topaz and metal is gold.

4. It represents a gentle tendency and sweet taste.

5. It represents fat constituents and tall height.

6. It indicates treasury, storeroom, and places where money and jewels are deposited.

7. It represents book shop, printing and stationery shop, educational institutions, financial institutions, charitable institutions.

8. It represents schools and colleges, teachers, professors, experts and advisors, department head and head of the institution.

9. It deals with medium clothes, living beings, and age of 30 years old.

10. It indicates Hemant season (20th Nov. to 19th Jan. approx.) and evenly momentum.

Profession: Jupiter gives success in subjects and professions related to Philosophy, Psychology, Vedas, Counselor, Financial Advisor, Bankers, Law, Treasury,

Literature, Judge, Lawyer, Editor, Professor, Teachers, Management, Directors, Priest, Astrologer, Administrator, Minister, Head of the department, Spokesperson, Cashiers, Scholars, Religious heads, Preachers, Priests, Vice-chancellors, Lecturers, Professional Experts, Judges, Advocates, etc.

Affliction: The afflicted Jupiter makes the person extreme and fanatic. It puts the person in the ocean of darkness and in the absence of knowledge, the person is not ready to listen to anyone. Because of his arrogant nature, he wanders here and there without any fruit. Afflicted Jupiter indicates false optimism, false faith, and orthodox beliefs.

A weak Jupiter indicates a lack of hope, absence of knowledge, greed, materialistic nature, extravagant, overconfident, lazy, worthless promises, etc. The native will not be a liberal person; instead of dutiful he will be careless. Show false reputation to others, shying away from religious activities, and chanting spiritual rhymes are very difficult for him. He will always do improper judgments and make mistakes in calculations.

5.6 Venus

Venus is considered a warm and rajasic planet. It represents a charming personality. Persons under its influence are kind and sociable. It rules over marriage and represents the wife in the male horoscope. It rules over all kinds of beauty, pleasures, and luxuries of life. It makes a person generous and cheerful. People under its influence are soft-spoken and they rarely show their anger on their face, when they are angry, they try to remain silent.

Being a feminine planet Venus presents feminine qualities. They are gentle people and show graceful manners, they avoid quarrels and turmoil at any cost, and try to lead a happy and peaceful life. They are caring by nature and take care of every member of the family. These people like to live in harmony with everyone. The person always prefers cleanliness in matters related to the house in which Venus is placed in the native's horoscope. For example, if Venus is in the Ascendant, then the person will take care of his clothes and like to eat quality food, such a person never accepts anything degraded.

Venus represents love and love demands attention. The relationship will dry and come to an end if you do not properly feed the relationship. In the same way, in which house Venus is placed, the activities related to the house require your attention. A favorable Venus indicates a good relationship with partners, easy negotiations, and a win-win situation.

Venus is tender and polite. It rules our senses and indicates laziness in a person. Under its influence, a person has a soft body and avoids doing laborious work. Such people like to relax all day, listen to music and avoid doing any productive work. Due to their strong senses, they can catch the subtle vibrations and like singing and dancing. Venus must be strong in a chart to make a good career in art and music, it gives a melodious and pleasing voice to the person.

Venus rules the semen and sexual energy of the human body. Through purification in the human body, blood is converted into sperm, and when a sperm is fertilized it turns into a newborn baby. Therefore, Venus is associated with diamonds. Just as a diamond attracts attention, a newborn baby attracts everyone's attention.

In every purification only the best moves forward, and the waste is removed. Whatever activity the purification process takes place in, it is controlled by Venus.

Therefore, Venus represents the best and Saturn represents the waste. For the seeker of truth, the whole world becomes waste, therefore, Saturn represents renunciation.

Venus indicates garnishing and has a special influence on clothing and adornments. It indicates makeup, fragrance, delicious food and luxury in life. If we analyze all these things in a subtle way, we know that all these things come through a process of refining, where the final product is tested many times. This is similar to the process of nature making diamonds from coal. Coal undergoes a difficult process of refining by withstanding pressure and heat for millions of years and becomes a diamond.

The outcome provided by Venus take time, everything that shines in life is controlled by Venus and the process of shining always takes time. Hence the place of diamond is forehead. It signifies the transformation of sexual energy into spiritual energy, which moves upwards and reaches the head.

Venus is the lord of Bharani, Purva Phalguni, and Purvashada nakshatras. These three nakshatras are located between Aries, Leo and Sagittarius. It shows that

Venusian energy never takes initiative and prefers to wait. A woman prefers to wait than taking initiative. Therefore, sexual energy never transforms on its own and it keeps waiting for the efforts of the seeker. This is also revealed by its symbol diamond, as it takes a lot of time to form but the result is beyond imagination. That is why every person wants Venus in their life.

Venus is exalted in the twelfth house and it is the house of salvation. The rotation of Venus in the opposite direction of Earth indicates the transformation of sexual energy into spiritual energy, it shows that when the sexual energy moves against the gravitational force of Earth i.e., upward, and reaches the Sahasrara Chakra (Crown Chakra), one will become enlightened. This is the reason why Venus is exalted in the house of Jupiter (the 12th house is the house of Jupiter and Jupiter considers Venus as its enemy). The debilitation of Venus in the 6th house indicates wastage of sexual energy.

Venus Represents:

1. It is a feminine, Brahmin caste planet and represents fresh water.

2. It represents film industry, cinema hall, photography, music, dancing room, bedroom, banquet, textiles, automobiles, cars, ships, airplanes, glass industry, confectionery, perfume, embroidery, milk, paint, sandal, soar fruits, jewellery, dress, vehicle, sexual pleasure, flowers, drinking water, hotels, honour, respect, female boss, business relation with females, catering, toys, delicious food, juice, drinks, etc.

3. Its colour is variegated and represents diamonds and pearls.

4. It represents excellent cloth and bedrooms.

5. Its taste is sour and the tendency is light.

6. It rules over all exotic vegetables, potatoes, cabbages, fruit trees, flower trees, creeping plants, and organic matter.

7. It represents the average height and age of 16 years old.

8. It indicates Vasant season and sideways momentum.

Profession: Venus gives success in profession related to Music, Dance, Arts, Poetry, Painting, Entertainment,

Media, Theatres, Interior designer, Fashion Designer, Actor, Singer, Model, Cosmetics, Textiles, Garments, Perfumes, Beauty-parlor, Stage performer, Furniture, Cartoonist, Personal Secretory, Receptionists, Florists, Handicrafts, Weaving, Sociology, Architect, Photographer, Gemstones, Web development, Animation, Advertisement, Hotel Management, Business relating to females, Catering, Receptionist, Private secretary, Salesperson, Counsellors, Party organizers and marriage-related work, Stage show, Actor, Comedian, Beauty parlour, Photography, Chemical, Sculpture, etc.

Affliction: An afflicted Venus indicates over-Indulgence in sexual activities, loss of a partner, separation from the beloved, excessive marriages, loss of prestige, scandals, fond of fancy food and overeating, company of bad friends, etc. A weak Venus indicates that such a person is deeply indulged in drinking alcohol, likes to enjoy his senses and is always in search of some frivolous pleasure.

An afflicted Venus denies the marriage, it indicates quarrels with the partner or a breakup in the relationship. The person will lead an immoral life, obsessed with desires, jealous, and vengeful. Accidents through animals and birds are also indicated by afflicted Venus.

5.7 Saturn

Saturn is an icy cold, windy and dry planet. This indicates that things become cold and dry when Saturn's influence begins. Once very warm relations, become cold; A hot business turns sluggish and things freeze like ice. According to Hindu astrology, Saturn is said to be 'lame' which indicates the slow movement of the planet. Due to the influence of Saturn, various activities start slowing down and things do not move as fast as they were earlier. The downward movement of Saturn indicates that it will bring down the person to earth and show the real truth of life.

Due to the Saturnine effect the person will always reach late, the journey will be delayed, projects will not complete on time. Airplanes, trains, and buses run late.

A strong Saturn indicates; honesty, reliability, truthfulness, balance in judgment, dutifulness, piousness, meditation, and concentration. Saturn bestows discipline, perseverance, responsibility, patience, endurance, stability, control, and frugality. Under the influence of Saturn, the person will grow a beard and do penance. It brings separation, silence, isolation, disease, old age, death, poverty, ugliness, and destruction.

Saturn is alert and careful; it rules over secret matters. It controls unfair judgment and brings balance. It brings limits and hates haste and works only after due consideration. Saturn is the protector and represents protection and security. A security guard must be tall and courageous. Persons under the influence of Saturn are tall and courageous.

Saturn is the son of the Sun but an enemy. Saturn is stubborn but does justice to everyone. Sun represents father and government. When there is a dispute between father and son or there is a problem with the government, then it is an indication of the relationship between Saturn and the Sun.

When a person is suffering from a period of despair or depression, then he goes into a dark room and reduces all hope, Saturn is darkness and despair. Therefore, to overcome such a situation, a person should not sit in a dark room with the lights off and he must remove all the negative energies around him. Saturn is isolation and filth; such persons will keep themselves in isolation and avoid cleaning their rooms and clothes. Saturn represents stale and cold foods; The person loses all interest in the food and starts eating stale food. Saturn is slow and lethargic; one loses all interest and becomes very slow in his daily activities. (Note: Readers can refer to my book 'Psychology and Investment' to know more about depression.)

People under the influence of Saturn prefer cold than hot. They prefer to eat ice cream than tea or coffee. They like to eat preserved foods, but remember Saturn is very stubborn. Excessive consumption of Saturnine products will make a person very stubborn. Each planet controls certain food items and by eating such a thing, such a planet gets strength.

Saturn creates; obstacles, impediments, hindrances and will make the way difficult for the native. Human nature is that whatever you get for free, you will not appreciate it. Saturn teaches hard lessons to the person so that he gives importance to whatever he has gained or achieved.

Saturn represents fog, mist, and dust. People influenced by Saturn think a lot and cannot decide what to do. A weak Saturn indicates that the person is unable to take the right decision, their mind is clouded and they cannot see a clear picture. In case of any wrong deeds, a weak

Saturnian person tries to spread dust on the matter and hide it, so that others also do not see a clear picture.

Saturn is exalted in Libra; Saturn represents balance and Libra is dance, the most desirable quality for dance is balance, it requires perfect balance. Everything on this earth is perfectly balanced and the dance of 'Nataraja' is going on continuously and the whole nature is presenting that dance that is perfectly balanced. Lord Saturn keeps balancing everything.

Libra is the marketplace and Saturn is honesty. The exaltation of Saturn indicates that the person will be honest in doing business. Exalted Saturn indicates that one will give an equal share to all without any bias. Libra is a symbol of companionship, Librans are generous and help others, Saturn is respect, partnership will last long when you respect and help your partner.

It indicates that the person will listen to the opinion of the public at large and will give importance to everyone's opinion and then will make a final decision, no one can influence the decision taken by Saturn. Aries represents single nature, while Libra represents partnership, these two zodiac signs are opposite to each other. Aries represents the singular soul and Saturn rules the masses.

The element of Aries does not support the nature of Saturn and it becomes debilitated in this sign.

The position of Saturn in the horoscope indicates delay and struggle in matters related to the respective house, but Saturn always fulfils his promises. The transit of Saturn brings changes in the life of a person. Saturn has the power to destroy all material desires of a person and shows the true picture of life that only death is certain in this world, a very strong Saturn makes a person a hermit.

Saturn Represents:

1. Its colour is blue, the metal is iron and lead, and the stone is sapphire.

2. It represents rags, torn clothes, and inorganic matter.

3. It represents machines, pumps, cement, bricks, chopped woods, coal and oil.

4. It represents masses and working-class people.

5. It governs the muscles, indicates a tall person, and is related to old age.

6. It is a shudra (servant) caste planet and its gender is eunuch.

7. Its taste is astringent and the tendency is hard.

8. It belongs to thorny and poisonous trees, broom, bitter gourd, onion, drumstick, betel leaves, tobacco, and greens.

9. Its season is Sisira (January-March) and the momentum is downward.

Profession: Saturn gives success in profession related to Oil & Gas, Iron & Steel, Metals & Mines, Real estate, Law, Labour & Servants, Municipality workers, Agriculture, Head of a labor union, Coffin maker, Cremation ground, Ice-maker, Cold storage, Preservatives, Geography, Archeology, Bricks, Tiles, Stones, Leather goods, Machines, Workshop, Wool, Quarries, etc.

Affliction: If Saturn is afflicted the native will become lethargic, idle, lazy. It indicates denial, depression, disharmony, disappointment, dejection, despondency, a difference of opinion, etc. If it is heavily afflicted the native will become a cruel criminal. This creates distortion and paranoia. Saturn is dark, afflicted Saturn indicates underworld activities, sexual perversions, and unnatural sexual activities. The native will do any harm to others for the fulfillment of his desire. The native feels pleasure by causing pain to others and will use any kind of violence.

5.8 The Lunar Nodes - Rahu and Ketu

According to mythology, Lord Vishnu beheaded a demon named Swarnabhanu while he was sitting by the side of the gods at the time of distributing amrita (nectar). At that time, Swarnabhanu knew that the gods were not going to fulfill their promise of equitable distribution of nectar. He changed his entire outfit, began to look like a deity, and sat on the side where the deity was sitting to drink the nectar.

But Sun and Moon recognized him that he is not a deity, he is a demon and they informed Lord Vishnu. Immediately Lord Vishnu beheaded him but before that, he had drunk a few drops of nectar. That's why he became immortal. His head is called Rahu and his headless body becomes Ketu. The energy of these nodes is strange and mysterious and they always move in retrograde motion.

In Indian astrology Sun, Earth and Moon; three planets are involved to create the energy of Rahu and Ketu. The ecliptic is an imaginary line on the sky that marks the annual path of the Sun. The movement of the Earth and the Moon on their path produces enormous energy. The motion of the Moon when intersects this path, disturbs this energy. When the Moon's orbit crosses the ecliptic to the north, that point of intersection is called Rahu. Ketu is the point 180° apart from that intersection. Thus, Rahu and Ketu are the two imaginary points without any shape. This intersection creates the disturbance of two massive energies, any planet near these nodes gets disturbed and creates unusual events in the life of the native.

When a planet in transit crosses these nodes in the birth chart, there is a disturbance in the matter related to the respective house.

Some scriptures say that Rahu is exalted in Taurus and debilitated in Scorpio and Ketu is vice-versa. While some other classics say that Rahu is exalted in Gemini and debilitated in Sagittarius. Rahu is the co-ruler of Aquarius and its Mooltrikona sign is Virgo, while Ketu is the co-ruler of Scorpio and its Mooltrikona sign is Pisces. Both nodes represent tall in height and age of 100 years.

5.8.1 Rahu

Rahu - the north node of the Moon is a shadowy planet. The direction of Rahu is South-West and stays 18 months in a sign. The caste of Rahu is Mleccha (outcaste) and it represents all foreign elements like a foreign land, foreign caste, foreign people, etc. Rahu represents those reptiles having poison in their mouths like snakes, while Ketu represents those insects and creatures having poison in tails like scorpions. Rahu's gemstone is Gomedha.

The above mythology is very important to understand the characteristic of Rahu. Like Swarnabhanu had an intense desire to drink the nectar at any cost. Rahu signifies passion and obsession. To achieve this burning desire, he changed his face, his clothes, left the side of demons, joined the side of devatas, and took big risks with only one goal or better we can say with only one obsession - "I want this nectar at any cost" and he achieved it. But after achieving this, he lost his body shape.

The behavior of the person having a strong influence on Rahu is also the same. They are extremely obsessed to achieve their desire. For that purpose, they can cross any limit and don't care about the outcome and suffering. Just as Swarnabhanu lost the shape of his body in the end, similarly a person following the path of his obsession has to lose a lot from his life. One day he will get what he wants but for that, he will have to pay a very high price, like Swarnabhanu paid the price.

Mythology says that the Sun and the Moon recognized the demon sitting by the side of the gods and informed Lord Vishnu. After that, Sun and Moon became strong enemies of Rahu and Ketu. Eclipse caused due to the transit of Rahu & Ketu and they have complete power to engulf Sun and Moon.

Sun and Moon represent our soul and mind. It means that if you run after your materialistic desire your soul and mind will become weak, your vision will become blurred and you will not be able to identify the truth. The smoke of materialism will gradually surround you and it will take over your soul and mind. But if your soul and mind are strong then you can recognize the illusion created by Rahu. The person who has strong Sun and Moon can easily catch the hidden motive of the mischievous persons and keep himself away from all these. This is one of the many reasons; we worship the

Sun and the Moon in Hindu culture so that our spirit and mind are strong and not eclipsed by material desire in the mundane world.

Rahu has only a mouth but no body. It indicates that a person with a strong influence of Rahu has a great desire but does not have the ability to digest it. Rahu always thinks about the future and its position in the horoscope indicates that the person wants to experience things that he does not have till now. Rahu means imbalance, mistakes; where a person learns from his experience. The Rahu-Ketu axis reflects the karmic balance that we carry from our past lives - what we did and what we want to achieve. Rahu is such a power that does not listen to anyone's advice and is ready to cross any limit to fulfill his intense desire. Such natives do not care about the result, even if their head is cut off like Swarnabhanu.

Rahu is an airy and lawless planet. Rahu does not like any boundaries. A person having a strong influence of Rahu behaves the same. They don't want any control over themselves, they are ready to break any rule, and sometimes their behavior is over expansive. They don't like any questions and they don't want to give any explanations. They wander here and there like air and waste their time and energy.

Rahu Represents:

1. Rahu indicates name, fame, overnight popularity, glamour, media sensation, material success, etc. All these represent illusion to the material world, and Rahu is the lord of all illusion.

2. Due to the effect of Rahu, the person will show his face to the world and become popular. It controls the film and cinema industry, advertising industry, all modern computers, television, etc., and those jobs where a person is showing their face to the masses.

3. Rahu represents smoke, materialism, drugs, dark, and poison. Rahu is subtle, insensitive, deceptive, telling lies, harsh and voluptuous planet.

4. Malefic Rahu indicates the person who will not think even twice of betraying his most trusted person. He can go to any extent to fulfill his desire.

5. Rahu indicates big machines, modern technology, technical works, poison and drugs, pesticides, chemicals, liquor, gambling and speculation, lottery, black magic, phobias, leprosy, giddiness, fear from unknow, insanity, smuggling, underworld activities, terrorists, etc.

6. Rahu is associated with import. People wait for their product, when they will receive their desired products in their hands. It indicates desire of the person, therefore, all activities related with import is controlled by Rahu.

7. Rahu represents paternal grandfather, quarrelsome person, greediness, cunningness, conspiracy, foreigners, skin diseases, indigestion, restlessness, swelling in the body, problem-related with gas.

8. Rahu means imbalance, mistakes; where a person learns from his experience.

11. Rahu is an airy and lawless planet.

12. Rahu is liar and want to achieve success without making any effort.

13. Rahu does not like any boundaries. A person having a strong influence of Rahu behaves the same.

14. Rahu doesn't want any control over themselves,

15. Rahu is ready to break any rule, and sometimes their behavior is over expansive. These people don't like any questions and they don't want to give any explanations.

Profession: Rahu gives success profession related to Poison, Medicines made from poison, Homeopathy, Researchers of medicine or drugs, Waste- material-dealers, Cosmetic surgeon, Smokes, Mobile, Technology, Environmental Science, Lawyer, Airlines, Sweepers, Detective, Magician, Anesthetist, Aeronautical Engineering, Astronomers, Wine sellers, Politics, Diplomacy, Speculation, Television, Innovation, and all non-conventional careers, Import-Related Activities, etc.

5.8.2 Ketu

Ketu - the south node, is the shadow planet of sudden and unexpected things. It also represents the experiences of our past lives, which we learned at a very high level and with mastery. It also represents a rigid and critical mindset where perfection is the highest goal at any cost. Ketu gemstone is Cat's eye also known as Lehsunia.

The symbol of Ketu is a flag that always stands vertically indicating the direction of the planet. A flag represents victory, but victory is not easy, victory on the battlefield is followed by great bloodshed and great sacrifices. The position of Ketu indicates that the native will get a victory after a lot of hard work and great sacrifice. Ketu provides clairvoyance and wisdom but after sufferings.

A strong Ketu blessed the native with powerful insights. It gives a power of intense concentration and deep penetration. This also represents vaccination where medicine is injected into the body. Ketu represents strong intuition, isolation, mediation, deep research, scientific jobs, drilling activities, etc.

It belongs to those jobs where a person does with full concentration, to achieve their goal the person leaves the rest of the world and forgets everything. A strong Ketu is necessary to sit in the meditation for long hours. Ketu is a planet of seclusion and has no interest in the material world, the higher aspect of Ketu is salvation (Moksha).

Ketu Represents:

1. Ketu represents Infra-Red Light, which is not visible to human eyes represents the mysterious functioning of this planet. It belongs to those diseases that are hidden and not easy to identify.

2. Ketu is related to spirituality, religious matters, astrology and other occult science.

3. Ketu is related to drugs and equipment, small gadgets, dogs, cattle breeding and farming.

4. Ketu indicates researchers, psychologists and healers.

5. Ketu belongs to hidden matters that are not easily identified.

6. Ketu provides power go to in deep because it has no vision to see the futility of mundane world.

7. Ketu belongs to those jobs where a person does with full concentration, to achieve their goal the person leaves the rest of the world and forgets everything.

8. Ketu denotes separation, in which Ketu is placed it indicates separation from all materialistic things related to that house.

9. Ketu is associated with export. It is a process of separation to the goods form its manufacturer. The producer has produced goods with their hard work but if he is able to convert it into money then there is no use of goods for him. He needs a buyer, who is ready to pay for that goods. The producer of the product has no

attachment with their product if someone is ready to pay for that. So, Ketu is related with all export related activities.

10. Ketu is a planet of sudden events; a person has to face sudden changes in his life related to the matter of the concerned house.

11. A malefic Ketu represents false sainthood, false knowledge, cheating, and humbugging profession, jealousy, hatred, deceit, murder, low-class sinful habits, etc.

12. These nodes indicate all hidden criminal, anti-social activities that are done mostly at night.

Profession: Ketu gives success profession related to Computers, Programming Language, Microbiologist, Saints, Detective, Secret affairs, Knowledgeable in the cryptic genre, Philosophy, Religion doctrines, Self-analysis, Occult, Palmists, Chemist, Preacher, Metaphysics, Export-Related Activities, etc.

5.9 Career by Signs

Aries: Military, Police, Surgeon, Firefighting, Athletes, Entrepreneur, etc.

Taurus: Music, Cosmetics, Luxury goods, Jewelry, Fashion, Money management, Teaching, Agriculture, Hospitality, etc.

Gemini: Media, Journalism, Public relations, Marketing, Broadcaster, Advertising, Accountants, Sales person, Translators, Writers, etc.

Cancer: Marine, Nursing, Hospitality, Human resources, Interior designing, Food, Restaurant, Home care, Child care, Personal secretary, Sailors, etc.

Leo: Corporate executive, Government jobs, Politics, Financial services, Investing, Speaker, etc.

Virgo: Accountant, Technician, Data scientists, Astrology, Media, Medical, Proof reader, Editor, Detective, Administrator, Forensic technician, Survey, Research work, etc.

Libra: Art, Dance, Architecture, Judges, Cosmetics, Fashion, Receptionists, Advertising, Interior decorating, Prostitutes, etc.

Scorpio: Chemicals, Drugs, Liquids, Insurance, Medical, Therapist, Detective, Body-guard, Investigator, Occult, Police, Research, etc.

Sagittarius: Religion, Banking and finance, Entrepreneurs, Sportsperson, Tour guide, Philanthropist, Correspondent, Coach, etc.

Capricorn: Logistics, Supply chain, Agent, Career Counsellor, Financial advisor, Administrator, etc.

Aquarius: Scientists, Inventors, Musicians, Designers, Consultants, Philosophers, Engineers, Computing, etc.

Pisces: Doctors, Nurses, Hospitals, Marine related, Charity worker, Film director, Counselors, Prisons, etc.

5.10 Career by Houses

First House: Self-employment, The body (gym), etc.

Second House: Banking, Investments, Finance, Teaching, Accountants, Food-related business, etc.

Third House: Communication, Writing, Publishing, Sales, Advertising, Travel, Import-export, etc.

Fourth House: Education, Agriculture, Vehicle, Real estate, Water, Mining, etc.

Fifth House: Speculation, Stock brokers, Entertainment, Creation, Self-expression, etc.

Sixth House: Health, Fitness, Labour, Police, Court, Loan recovery, Clinics, etc.

Seventh House: Partnership in business, Females, Foreign business, etc.

Eighth House: Insurance, Research, Secret, Occult, Sex, Cremation, etc.

Ninth House: University, Higher education, Religion, Teaching, Long travel, Head of the temple, etc.

Tenth House: Public life, etc.

Eleventh House: Group work, Side ventures, etc.

Twelfth House: Foreign, Hospitals, Prisons, Charities, etc.

Chapter 6

Important Factors to Consider for Business

There are many benefits associated with business but on the other hand there are many risks also associated with it. Every job has its own boundaries where the person has to work within them but in business the person is the boss himself. But facing business challenges is not easy. It requires the ability to understand the risks associated with the business and take timely preventive measures.

Many businesses fail due to not taking proper decisions, not understanding changing circumstances, greed, etc.

Therefore, various skills are required to run a successful enterprise. In this chapter we will discuss various aspects related to business according to astrology.

6.1 Significator for Business

i. Ascendant: Analyze the ascendant and the position of the ascendant lord in the horoscope. (Already discussed in Chapter 4.)

ii. Mercury: Mercury is an important planet for business and trade activities. Business requires intelligence and timely decision making and a strong Mercury provides all these qualities. Mercury rules communication which is important in business.

iii. Rahu: Rahu indicates desire; desire for money which provides freedom to do what the person want to do, desire to become own boss, desire to break limitations and make own rule, desire to achieve success at any cost. Rahu is a disturbed energy and always hungry.

iv. Saturn: Strong Saturn represents a disciplined person who always follows his words. Such persons like to work hard to get success in life.

Check the relationship of Lagna lord, Mercury, Rahu and Saturn with the 3rd, 7th, 10th and 11th houses. Strong relationships between them are good for business.

6.2 Different Combinations for Business

i. The 2nd, 6th and 10th houses are known as earth trikona houses and earth is the significator of resources. Strong earth houses mean that the person will not face problem of resources in his life. Find out the connection of 3rd house with earth trikona house.

ii. Find out the connection between 3rd house and ascendant and its lord. Such a person has ability to take courageous decisions in life.

iii. Find out the connection between 3rd house and 10th and 11th house. 10th is for karma and 11th is for income. Any connection between these houses produces favorable results.

iv. The lord of 9th house from D1 chart should be strong in D9 chart.

v. Position of 10th lord from D1 chart is important in D10 chart. It is good for business if it placed in 3rd, 7th and 11th house. The 3rd house is related with enterprise, the 7th

house is related with business and partnership, the 11th house is related with friends, colleagues and resources. It is the house of income and gains, without resources there is no gains. So, in D10 chart, the 11th house indicates availability of resources for business.

vi. Fixed signs (Taurus, Leo, Scorpio, Aquarius) play a vital role in business. When the lord of the tenth house in D1 chart is placed in a fixed sign in D10 chart then success in business is assured.

vii. It is important to consider the position of Venus in D1 and D10 chart. Venus indicates private sector and Mercury is related with all trading activities. Therefore, conjunction or aspect or placement of Venus and Mercury is good for business.

viii. Check the position of 2nd and 11th house in D1 chart. The 2nd house is for savings, and 11th house if for gains. A relation between the two produces favorable results and the person can save his income.

6.3 Mercury Retrograde

Financial decisions are very important in everyone's life. We should be extremely careful while making any such decision. But sometimes people make wrong decisions.

For example;

i. Wrong investment even after a lot of research and consideration,

ii. Wrong purchase of a property and subsequent legal battle,

iii. Wrong online payment,

iv. Wrong booking and its payment,

v. Wrong decision due to misunderstanding or loss of communication, etc.

It is important to understand finance but financial astrology also has great importance which many people are not aware of. One such is Mercury retrograde, because Mercury rules the movement of money, investments, banking, finance, etc. It rules all modes of communication which can easily go awry during the retrograde period. Therefore, it is not good to take career, investments and important business decisions when Mercury is retrograde.

Mercury completes one cycle of the Sun in 88 days and is retrograde for a maximum of 25 days. Many people make financial mistakes when Mercury is retrograde.

6.4 Important Yogas

There are many important yogas in astrology and the native's horoscope should promise some strong yogas, without that success in the material world is difficult. It is important to consider these yogas in D1 and D9 chart both, because D9 chart represents our fortune and every person fortune pulls him. Yogas present in D1 chart are associated with the birth of the person whereas yogas present in D9 chart give their results in due course of time. Readers can refer to my book "Vedic Astrology: Light of Wisdom" to know some important yogas in the horoscope. Like; Dhana yoga, Pancha-Mahapurush Yoga, Raj Yoga, Lakshmi yoga, etc.

6.5 Eclipse

Eclipse plays an important role in every person's life. At the time of eclipse positive energy disappears and negative energy gets activated. So, it is not good to take any financial decision at the time of eclipse. This is the time of uncertainty, so it is good to wait to stabilize the energy. The effect of solar eclipse is more important than lunar eclipse. One week before and after the solar eclipse are very crucial. There is a high probability that business started at the time of eclipse may face hurdles and closure.

Chapter 7

Role of Atmakaraka

According to Jaimini astrology, the karaka is of great importance and it varies for each horoscope. Karaka means factor, significator or agent. The determination of the karaka is based on the longitude of the planet from the beginning of the respective sign.

7.1 Atmakaraka

This is the planet having the highest longitude in a sign. The strength of this planet reflects the general strength of the horoscope. The natural Atmakaraka is considered the Sun. For example; suppose among all planets the Moon has the highest longitude is 27 degrees in Aries. So, Moon is considered as an Atmakaraka in this horoscope.

Sun represents soul, and every soul has done various good and bad deeds and the responsibility of all of them comes in this life. The imprint of all those deeds is present on the soul and the Atmakaraka planet represents it.

There is a definite purpose for a planet to be an Atmakaraka planet. It indicates that the soul has done various karmas (deeds) related to that planet, hence, it is the most karmic planet and the person is responsible for all his karmas. The Atmakaraka planet experiences the maximum amount of karma, the incomplete obligations of the person become a burden and every person has to bear the burden of his karma. It is the continuation of journey which we left in our past birth. Hence, the information about these seven karakas provides useful information about the person and among them Atmakaraka is the most important and is considered as the King.

A strong king is required to run a kingdom and he is surrounded by a good team of advisors. Therefore, an Atmakaraka planet should be strong in the horoscope and receive positive aspect of his supporting planets. A weak and poorly placed Atmakaraka indicates that the native is unable to take decisions and aspect of malefic planets create hamper in life.

It is important to consider in which Nakshatra the Atmakaraka is placed, because, the journey of this life will start from where it was left in the previous life. If the Atmakaraka is placed at Gandanta, it means that a new beginning in this life is waiting for the person, because Gandanta is a boiling point and the planet feels highly uncomfortable at this place. Neither a person nor the planet wants to stay at the boiling point.

Mahadev Pathaka in Jataka Tatva has written (T-36) that during the Bhukti of Atmakaraka planet, the person falls from his position and there is a possibility of loss.

7.2 Qualities of Atmakaraka

Before making any decision, it is necessary to identify the Atmakaraka planet in the horoscope because it plays an important role in the decision taken by the person. Following are some of the qualities of a planet when it is Atmakaraka.

i. Sun: The native has leadership abilities and the courage to walk alone on unknown paths. Such natives are creative and have the ability to take risks. But this also makes the natives arrogant. Such a person becomes proud of his position and wealth. Arrogance creates heat and heat gives birth to separation. Therefore, these people should learn humility in life.

ii. Moon: The native is receptive and compassionate. Moon is considered a mother, so the native has caring qualities. Strong Moon indicates the power of imagination and the person can excel in those works where such skills are required.

iii. Mars: Such a person is courageous, passionate, and adventurous by nature. The planet of war and weapons does not think twice before taking any steps. Therefore, such a person should avoid all kinds of violence. Yoga, spiritual development, and martial arts also require the energy of Mars. Consequently, they should use it only for creative purposes.

iv. Mercury: The native is strong in communication and networking. He is an intelligent person, has many friends, and is good at writing and editing. He is adaptable, witty, and diplomatic.

v. Jupiter: The native is a very knowledgeable person. He takes an interest in religious activities and is skilled in giving advice. He is a truthful and honest person and is respected as a Guru or Head.

vi. Venus: The native is interested in art and music, and likes cleanliness everywhere. Being a female planet, the native represents feminine qualities and shows manners and etiquette in life.

vii. Saturn: The native is very hardworking, honest and just. He is a responsible and disciplined person but has to face many challenges in life.

7.3 Atmakaraka with other Planets in Navamsha

Atmakaraka planet influenced by the planet placed in the same sign. Jaimini Sutras further explains the result of Atmakaraka with other Planets in Navamsha.

i. Atmakaraka with the Sun - The person will work in government service and political activities.

Note: Sun indicates government and if Sun is Atmakaraka or is related to Atmakaraka Sun then it indicates the native's involvement in government work or activities.

ii. Atmakaraka with Full Moon and Venus - The person will live a comfortable life with luxuries and will work as an educationist by profession.

Note: Strength of Moon indicates strength of mind and full moon indicates a person with stable mind and Venus bestows the person with luxuries.

iii. Atmakaraka with Mars - The native works as a metalist and possesses expertise in arms, weapons and products related with metal. He will do a profession related with fire, chemical and drugs.

Note: Work related with heat and fire can be seen here, like engine drivers, cooks and weapon makers who prepare various chemicals to change the quality of metal.

iv. Atmakaraka with Mercury - The native work as a trader, businessman, weaver or sculptor. Such a person is gentle in behavior and proficient in social activities.

Note: Mercury provides business acumen to the person and a strong Atmakaraka indicates strong understanding for business.

v. Atmakaraka with Jupiter - The native takes deep interest in religious activities. He is a righteous, knowledgeable, person and well versed in Vedas and scriptures.

Note: Jupiter indicates knowledge and wisdom, and association of Atmakaraka indicates that the planet bestows the person with such qualities.

vi. Atmakaraka with Venus – Such a person is a political figure or works as a government official. He is a passionate person, loves many women and lives for 100 years.

Note: Venus represents the desire for sexual pleasure and this passion remains in the person for a long time.

vii. Atmakaraka with Saturn – Saturn gives success in the chosen activity and as a result the person becomes famous.

Note: The fame given by Rahu does not last long but the fame given by Saturn lasts for ages. Saturn indicates struggle; hence the person will achieve success after a lot of struggle. Saturn elevates the person to a higher position and bestows success and fame.

viii. Atmakaraka with Rahu – Such a person produces bows and arrows. He earns his livelihood by stealing or deceiving. He deals with poisons and dangerous chemicals. He works in the field of medicine and is excellent in the work of iron and steel and other manufacturing industries.

Note: Rahu indicates work related to big machinery. Such a person can easily handle large machinery and other equipment related to iron and steel. Bows and arrows indicate guns, bullets and other warlike instruments. Stealing means that he is skilled in doing work without others knowing and deceiving indicates use of malpractices in the related work.

ix. Atmakaraka with Ketu - Such a person earns his livelihood with or through elephants, he may be a thief.

Note: Elephant is a peaceful animal, it indicates silently engage in doing a big task and a thief indicates act of doing such things without being notice of others. Association with Ketu indicates a person who silently engages in his activities and don't like to be noticed by others.

7.4 Karakamsha

Where the Atmakaraka planet is situated in Navamsha, that zodiac sign is called Karakamsha. Wherever the lord of Karakamsha is situated in the natal horoscope that zodiac sign is made the ascendant of the Karakamsha horoscope and the remaining planets change their houses accordingly.

For example; In D1 chart, the planet with the highest longitudinal degree is Moon. Find the position of Moon in D9 chart; suppose it is placed in Gemini, then Gemini is called Karakamsha.

To prepare Karakamsha chart, find in which sign the lord of Gemini i.e. Mercury is situated in D1 chart, suppose it is situated in Sagittarius, make Sagittarius the Karakamsha ascendant and move the rest of the planets.

Atmakaraka planet is the karaka of soul, hence Karakamsha chart tells more about the soul and the individual.

Chapter 8

The 10th House

The zodiac moves one after the other towards the horizon, changing every two hours and rising again in the east about 24 hours later. Hence, the position of the Sun in a horoscope indicates the time of birth of the person. When the Sun is at its highest point it is known as Midheaven or Medium Coeli (MC) and in a horoscope, the 10th house represents this point.

The Sun touches the mid-sky point every day at noon, so it is at the highest angle of heaven. This house is directly above the earth at one's birth. It is opposite the Nadir Point or IC which is represented by the 4th house.

Sun means activity and when the Sun reaches its highest point, the activities are more and this is represented by the 10th house. Therefore, this is the house of karma and the activities and inconsistencies associated with it are highly visible. This house represents the profession, career, and social status of the individual. It is related to the public life, ambition, and achievements of the individual. This house also shows our relationship with superiors, bosses, and authorities.

To determine one's career 2nd, 6th, and 10th house should be analyzed carefully because these are earthy signs and represent material gains. A strong 10th house is necessary for a successful career in life. The transit of Saturn through this house indicates the high worldly activities of the natives.

A person's profession is the total of his entire personality and he is motivated to do only that work for which he has the ability, qualities, and skills. Every human being reaps the fruits of his own actions, so for a career, it is necessary to examine the planets placed in the tenth house, the aspects of other planets, and the position of their lord.

To decide a person's career, we must consider every aspect of the horoscope. In this chapter, we will examine the role of the tenth house.

8.1 Source of Livelihood

Every person derives his livelihood according to his inner nature and this is achieved through the position of the planets in the 10th house and its lords. Strong planets determine which livelihood is most suitable for the person. Therefore, the 10th house and its lord play a vital role in determining the profession of the individual. However, the Lagna and the 6th house should also be considered.

Phaladeepika by Mantreswara's states that, "The strongest planet situated in the 10th house from the Lagna or the Moon helps in acquiring wealth." (Chapter 5)

The source of acquisition of wealth;

i. If the planet be the Sun – Father

ii. If the planet be the Moon – Mother

iii. If the planet be Mars – Enemy

iv. If the planet be Mercury - Friend

v. If the planet be Jupiter - Brother

vi. If the planet be Venus – Wife

vii. If the planet be Saturn - Servant

The native will undertake the profession which is assigned to the lord of the Navamsa, occupied by the lord of the 10th house from the Lagna, from the Moon and the Sun (distinctively), whichever is the strongest.

Example: The ascendant is in Cancer; The Sun is in Virgo and the Moon is in Libra. The 10th lord Mars also is in Libra at 15:56:36. In D9 chart Mars falls in Aquarius navamsha which lord is Saturn. So, we can consider that Saturn is the main significator for source of livelihood for this native.

Note: A person's livelihood is not determined by only one planet. In the present world it is a combination of many qualities of the person. So, we cannot ignore the planets from Sun and Moon. A person's livelihood is also affected by these planets, but the condition is that they should be strong and should not be in Dusthana Bhava (6th, 8th and 12th).

The Sutra further states;

i. If the lord of Navamsa is strong then wealth will be obtained without any obstacle or exertion.

ii. If it is weak, very little wealth is earned.

iii. The country from which the money will be accrued is indicated by the sign of the 10th house or the Navamsha of the lord of the 10th house.

iv. If the sign be occupied or aspected by its lord, then the source of income will be in his own country. This will also happen when the Lord of the tenth house is in a fixed sign in the Navamsa.

v. If the sign of the tenth house be occupied or aspected by planet other than its lord, then the native will earn money at a place other than his own country.

8.2 Wisdom from Ancient Scriptures

8.2.1 Hora Sara

Hora Sara written by Prithuyasas states that, "If no planet situated in the 10th house than 10th from the Sun and the Moon and in which sign the 10th lord is situated should be considered."

The lord of the Navamsha occupied by the strongest 10th lord counted from the Ascendant, the Sun or the Moon plays an important role in deciding the career of a person.

8.2.2 Saravali

The 10th house counted from the strongest among the ascendant (Lagna) and the Moon is called Karmasthana. If the lord of the 10th house is strong then the influence in relation to karma will increase, otherwise it will decline. Therefore, strongest among the two decides the earnings of the person.

8.2.3 Phaladeepika

If Saturn is in the tenth house then the native will be a king or his minister, he will contribute to agriculture, will be courageous, wealthy and prestigious.

8.2.4 Sarvarth Chintamani

Sarvarth Chintamani written by Vyankatesh Sharma states that "Karma, ruling power, fame, rain, living away, works of public utility, honor, occupation, knees and servants should be considered from the 10th house."

Sarvarth Chintamani further states "If the 10th lord is weak and under the influence of malefic planets, this combination creates problems in work. When the 10th lord, Jupiter, and Mercury are strong, the native remains engaged in serving others. When these three planets are strong and aspected by benefics, they make the native particularly inclined to help in public works. But if they are in the 6th, 8th, or 12th house, badly aspected by malefic then such works are absent."

8.3 Karaka of the 10th House

There are four Karakas (significators) of the tenth house - Mercury, Sun, Saturn, and Jupiter. To earn money a person must have skills. Hence, Mercury represents skills and Saturn represents hard work. Sun represents the employer and Jupiter represents income. Among all four planets, Mercury is the prominent karaka of the 10th house because without any skill earning is difficult.

Mercury represents the childhood state and during that age children learn quickly. As the age grows learning becomes difficult because ego starts accumulating. Therefore, it becomes difficult for an egoistic person to develop new skills. Children are flexible, so the first criterion to learn is to become humble. So, the strength of Mercury is important for a successful career in life. Higher learning means higher growth. The other three planets must be strong and have a good relationship with the 10th house to produce favorable results.

8.4 Planets in the 10th House

A person works all day with the aim of earning money. Therefore, the tenth house is related to the reputation and social status of a person. A strong tenth house and the placement of its lord is essential for a successful career in life. Now we will discuss the presence of various planets in the tenth house.

8.4.1 Sun in the 10th House

The Sun in the 10th house indicates that career success comes easily in their life as the Sun is strong here and it has directional strength (Digbala) which indicates administrative qualities to the person. The maturity age of the Sun is 22 years; hence, these people start their careers around this age. They work very hard to shine in their career and turn adverse circumstances in their favor. Sun represents time; therefore, time is always important for them. They are always alert towards their work and complete it on time.

Sun indicates heat and more heat creates isolation. Strong Sun indicates an official position where the person sits alone and stays away from others. They are highly active individuals and work in key positions in government departments where their decisions affect many people. They want to be in the limelight and show their talent to the world. As their karma comes out, one day their bad karma also comes out. Sun is here and nothing related to the 10th house can remain hidden.

Saravali says, "If the Sun is in the tenth house then the native is very intelligent, wealthy, strong, has vehicles, relatives, sons, is successful in his work, valiant, invincible and great."

Affliction: An afflicted Sun indicates that they do not mind using unfair means in life to achieve success. It is important for them to be in the limelight, so they put their face forward in everything they do. They become egoistic and want credit for every work.

The word "I" becomes very important to them and appears in abundance in their conversations. Ego creates heat and heat creates distance, so people start avoiding them. They do not want to leave their post at any cost and as soon as they leave their post, they fall seriously ill.

8.4.2 Moon in the 10th House

The Moon represents our minds, emotions, and creativity. The light of the moon depends on the light of the sun. This means that such a person is diligent in following the orders of his superiors. The Moon in the 10th house makes the person engage in such work where the person takes instructions from others to follow them. A strong moon indicates high quality of creativity and imagination and the person engages in those work where these qualities are required. These people are good at writing because it requires a strong power of imagination.

Moon indicates public image, so they are always cautious about their image and engage in all those work where nurturing qualities are important. Moon gets directional weakness in the 10th house, hence the position of the Moon is not considered good here. They get easily panic and logic does not work on such people because emotions dominate them. They are easily swayed and make wrong decisions.

Saravali says, "If Moon is in the tenth house then the native is not unhappy, is dutiful, successful in his works, wealthy, pious, very strong, valorous and charitable."

Affliction: If the Moon is weak, poorly placed, or aspected by inauspicious planets, then the person's mind is easily influenced by external factors. A weak Moon indicates inconsistency, instability, and negativity.

One should keep in mind the element in which the moon is placed in this house. If the moon is placed in the water element, it shows that the person is unable to make firm decisions and is always in a dilemma. Such people are unable to digest criticism and get restless quickly. I have seen that such people are unable to control their minds and get nervous quickly.

8.4.3 Mars in the 10th House

Mars gets directional strength (digbala) in the 10th house, hence, its placement is considered good for career and professional success. These people are ambitious and desirous to achieve great things in life. They accept challenges and never run away from situations. They are bold, courageous, and aggressive people. Mars indicates physical activity and the 10th house indicates knee. They are a highly energetic person and accept those jobs where high physical activity is involved. The knees of these people are very strong and they engage in those activities where running is important. They perform better with sales and marketing, sports, physical activity, construction work, police, military, etc.

They are impulsive and impatient persons and keep running here and there to achieve their goals. Due to their daring attitude, they take risks in their career. When others shy away from doing a difficult task, they accept the challenge because Martian energy never sits silently. Hence, it is necessary to consider the aspect of Jupiter on Mars because Jupiter provides direction.

When energy gets direction it produces fruitful results, without direction energy goes in vain. In those houses where Jupiter and Mars simultaneously aspects, the person takes the right decision because energy gets direction. It indicates a career in engineering and technology.

Saravali says, "If Mars is in the 10th house then the native will be skillful in his work, valiant, invincible, will serve important people, will be blessed with sons and happiness and will be very courageous."

Affliction: They are very aggressive and demanding person in their professional life. If Mars is weak or aspected or conjunct by malefic then they are very impulsive and adopt unfair means. They are very desirous people and do not bother about doing wrong things to achieve their objective. They show their energy and power worthlessly to others.

8.4.4 Mercury in the 10th House

Mercury is a planet of communication and networking and the person has natural qualities in these fields. It indicates the intelligence, reasoning, and analytical abilities of the person. It provides diplomatic skills and qualities of negotiations and the person achieves success in these fields. Strong mercury bestows the person with multi-tasking abilities, it makes the person witty and the person can do sharp analysis with his intelligence.

Mercury is related to business, if other things are favorable then the person does his own business or self-earning through an independent profession. It deals with trade and commerce and the person is good at understanding finance.

Saravali says, "If Mercury is in the 10th house then the native will be of exceptional intelligence, perform distinguished tasks, be successful in his works, be very learned, courageous, strong and adorned with various kinds of ornaments."

Affliction: Intelligence is like a double-edged sword and Mercury represents the childhood stage. So, if Mercury is afflicted by the malefic planet then the person uses his intelligence to harm others. They are cheaters, fraudsters, hackers who use their skills to deceive others. A sword in the hands of a child is dangerous, it should always be under control of elders. So, it is necessary to consider the conjunction and aspect of other planets on Mercury. The benefic planet gives good results while the malefic planet gives birth to a person with negative thinking who wants instant money without any effort.

8.4.5 Jupiter in the 10th House

Jupiter indicates a successful career with literary pursuits. Such a person can easily get a job. The profession includes; Teaching, Banking, Financial Advisor, Publications, Government Advisor, Minister, Head of Department, Priest, etc. Jupiter makes a person very honest, loyal, and responsible. They are highly dedicated people and work is worship for them.

They work in an important position and their actions are easily noticed. They are broad-minded person, bring optimism, and hold key positions in organizations. When Mahadasha and Antardasha of Jupiter come, their career shines. The placement of Jupiter in this house makes a person wealthy, it provides a peaceful home and a pleasant and cordial workplace.

The tenth house on body parts represents the knee, which supports the movement and ability to handle pressure. Jupiter indicates they have a strong ability to handle work pressure and do not get frustrated easily.

Saravali says, "If Jupiter is in the 10th house then the native will be successful in his work, will be respectable, hardworking and will be blessed with abundant prosperity, happiness, wealth, relatives, vehicles and fame."

Affliction: On the downside, such a person may face work-life balance problem. Jupiter expands the workplace and creates an imbalance in other aspects of life.

8.4.6 Venus in the 10th House

Venus represents a charming personality. It is a feminine planet that has gentle qualities. They are very creative people and have excellent etiquette and manners, soft skills, and interpersonal qualities. They have artistic qualities and make a career in this field. They can excel in the fashion and entertainment industry, art and beauty, music and dance, etc.

Venus attracts the attention of everyone, Venus in the 10th house indicates that these people come into the limelight in their profession. They have a desire for social recognition and work hard to achieve it. Venus is a sensual planet, so the senses of these people are very strong. Venus is a lazy planet, so these people prefer every comfort in their life and a sort of laziness is reflected in their personality.

Saravali says, "If Venus is placed in the 10th house, the native will be successful in litigation and will be blessed with pleasure, sexual relations, honour, wealth, fame and great wisdom."

Affliction: Instead of working hard to achieve their goals, frivolous entertainment, and pleasure become their top priority. They use unethical means to achieve success and use their skills to charm others to fulfill their desire.

8.4.7 Saturn in the 10th House

When we work for someone, there is an owner of that work who hires people according to his needs and pays them in exchange for the work. According to the theory of Karaka, Sun represents the employer and Saturn represents efforts and labour. In astrology, Saturn is the most powerful of all the nine planets and it is the god of justice and has the power to punish anyone. There is no planet greater than Saturn as it is the lord of death that rules over every living being. When Saturn is in the tenth house, conflict begins between the employer and the employee. Therefore, the career of such a person is unstable and inconsistent.

- Sun means activity, when Sun comes the activity starts. Saturn slows down, freezes, and stops every activity.

- Sun represents ego and Saturn destroys every ego.

- Saturn can never accept the authority of the Sun.

- Sun and Saturn both are enemies and Saturn cannot work under the Sun.

The employer wants the employee to work under his control but the employee whose Saturn is in the 10th house cannot accept any wrong order given by the employer, he immediately challenges it. This situation becomes even more serious when Saturn aspects the 10th house in transit. I have seen that in this transit the tension between the employee and his boss intensifies and one of the two has to leave the organization.

This is not a normal situation when we consider the career prospects of the person. Stress and conflict become a part of their professional life and these people have to face many hurdles at the start of their career. They have to face conflict with their boss and even get fired from the organization. Two opposite energies cannot exist in one place, where one is visible and the other is invisible. Saturn is the lord of death that comes in every life one day. So, Saturn indicates the end. In the tenth house it indicates the end of the job, so one day such a person leaves the job forever.

But this is not the end of the career. The hard work of the person never goes in vain and being the planet of justice Lord Saturn always fulfills his promises. The placement of Saturn in the tenth house forces the person to work independently. So, such a person cannot work for others in his entire life. After doing a job for some time, the destiny of the person pulls him to become the master of his own work.

Freedom of action is seen from the tenth house and Saturn in the tenth house indicates that the native has the freedom to take decisions even if he is in a job. Hence, they work in responsible and senior positions where they are free to take all their decisions.

Saturn brings struggle and pressure in professional life and being a slow-moving planet, it delays career growth but brings success after struggle. Saturn creates distance, so these people prefer a job where they can work independently without any interruption. One day Saturn rewards the person with the fruits of their hard work and they get respect and appreciation for their endurance, perseverance and honesty.

In Napoleon Bonaparte's horoscope, Saturn was placed in the 10th house along with Mercury in Cancer sign. This gave him sudden rise in his military career but also his downfall.

Saravali says, "If Saturn is in the 10th bhava, the native will be wealthy, learned, courageous, a minister or judge, or will be the leader of a group, city or village."

Affliction: They are very conservative about their thoughts and behavior. They are stubborn, think that they are supreme, and are never ready to compromise under any circumstances. They adopt an orthodox approach, stick with their old principles, and are never ready to accept change.

8.4.8 Rahu in the 10th House

Rahu in the tenth house indicates that the person is hungry for professional success in life. They speak well and can impress others with their style and behavior. Such persons will take up jobs where showing face is important, like spokesperson, TV anchor, etc. They are known by many and public image is important to them. These people pursue unconventional careers or are associated with innovation and technology.

Rahu is a turbulent energy, matters related to the house it is placed in are always disturbed. Rahu in the tenth house indicates uncertainty and instability in professional life. So, these people should not do anything that may cause disruption, their actions may backfire.

Affliction: Rahu is always hungry, in the 10th house it indicates a person who is obsessed with work. For some reason, these people always prefer to stay away from their home and it is difficult for them to maintain a balance between work and life. Such persons do not hesitate to use any unfair means to achieve success.

8.4.9 Ketu in the 10th House

Ketu is the planet of separation and has no attachment to the matters of that house where it is placed. In the 10th house, Ketu brings an unstable career and suddenly separates the person from his work. These people do not take an interest to come in the limelight and prefer to sit in their own secluded place. They have strong power to go deep in any matter and are never satisfied by superficial observation of anything. Ketu indicates intuition power. Therefore, they find whatever is hidden and what is the true intention of the other person. These people are good in research, drilling, and those types of work where doing deep is involved.

Ketu in the 10th house indicates detachment from worldly pursuits, therefore, they learn occult science and take an interest in spirituality. These people love to do research and investigation but have no attachment to their workplace. A headless planet indicates that the action taken by the person no one knows.

Affliction: Sometimes their behavior becomes uncontrolled and they do unexpected and irregular things without any reason. They hide their actions and know how to get away with doing wrong things.

8.5 Placement of the 10th Lord in Different Houses

It is necessary to determine the direction of a career from multiple dimensions. Not only the planets in the 10th house but also the placement of the 10th lord in the D1 and D10 chart plays an important role in deciding the career. Now, we will examine the placement of the 10th lord in the D1 chart in different houses.

8.5.1 10th Lord in the 1st House

The 1st house indicates self, and the placement of the 10th lord in the 1st house suggests personality and profession are interrelated like a fashion model, dancer, soldier, etc. Prestige and public esteem are important for them and they are always cautious about that. They are cautious about their appearance and select their cloths carefully. These natives have strong character and are respected for their work. They have leadership qualities and attain significant positions in the organization (if other planets are strong).

8.5.2 10th Lord in the 2nd House

The second house represents family and tradition. The placement of the lord of the tenth house in the second house indicates that the person is involved in his family business or similar activities. Family is always important for them and they take care of their family members. They follow the tradition of family and the footsteps of elder members. The second house represents food and savings, so they are involved in work related to savings, catering, and business related to food items. This indicates that the person will earn money to feed his family members and arrange food for them (he may be the sole earner).

8.5.3 10th Lord in the 3rd House

It is the house of courage and transportation. The placement of the tenth house lord in the third house indicates the enterprising nature of the person. Such a person dares to move in an unknown direction. It is the house of communication and the person has excellent communication skills. They do jobs where daily travel is important. They take short trips to get their work done. Hence, it is related to sales and marketing, journalism, writing, YouTube videos, networking, courier services, etc.

8.5.4 10th Lord in the 4th House

When the Lord of Karma Bhava sits in the 4th house, then the person prefers to work from home or work in a place where work and home are together or make a room in his own house as an office. For example, working at a construction site or a factory where the person lives in a temporary house there. This means that the person's work and his living place are interrelated. Such people prefer to rent a house near their workplace. Family always plays an important role in the success of their professional life.

8.5.5 10th Lord in the 5th House

When the lord of the Karma Bhava sits in the fifth house which is the house of creativity, the interest or hobby of such a person becomes his career. All our hobbies and creativity are nothing but the accumulation of all our karmas and those karmas force us to act. Happiness and enjoyment are important for these people so they actively participate in recreational activities. This is the house of change in job or profession. Planets placed in this house indicate that the person will leave his job or change the profession and take up a completely new profession.

8.5.6 10th Lord in the 6th House

When the lord of the Karma Bhava sits in the daily work, routine, and service Bhava, then the person does such work in which it is important to follow the daily routine. This is the Bhava of struggle and competition and the person gets involved in such work where he has to deal with new problems day by day. Every day is a new day and every day creates a new struggle and new competition. Such a person never gets disappointed with any problem and also inspires others to struggle.

- It is the house of disease, so they deal with different types of diseases on a daily basis and work as a doctor.

- It is the house of conflict, so they deal with different types of conflicts on a daily basis and work as a lawyer.

- They work as a banker, customer service person, and sales representatives, where they meet new people and face new situations every day.

They are very busy people and work hard to fulfill their responsibilities. The 6th house must be strong for success in the job, so it is important to check not only the planets in the 6th house but also the position of the lord of the 6th house.

8.5.7 10th Lord in the 7th House

When the lord of the 10th house sits in the 7th house, the person is highly dedicated to his work. This is the house of marriage and partnership, such a person is interested in marriage and partnership-related matters and is extremely busy with work. His family members feel as if he is married to his work. Such people are good at building relationships with others and engage in activities where building new relationships is important.

Every marriage has its responsibilities and obligations and not everything is in writing. But in a materialistic deal, it has to be put in writing. So, these people are involved in preparing contract notes, agreement papers, legal documents, partnership papers, etc. so that the both- parties can understand and perform their responsibilities well and they are legally bound to do so. So, they are well versed with the law. They advise others and work as marriage counselors, legal counselors, and problem solvers between two parties. They work as mediators and people prefer to discuss with them for solutions.

8.5.8 10th Lord in the 8th House

When the lord of the tenth house is placed in the house of secret matters, hidden things, transformation, investigation, research, and mysterious things, the profession of the person is also influenced by these qualities. Such people take an interest in investigation and secret matters and they work as journalists, investigators, detectives, etc. They have confidential information and they keep it to themselves and deal when the time comes.

The eighth house is the house of sudden things, so they work in emergencies or a place where supply has to be made immediately when demand arises and they do their work with full responsibility. They take an interest in psychology, astrology, and occult things and increase their knowledge about occult sciences. The house of transformation indicates that change in their career is inevitable.

8.5.9 10th Lord in the 9th House

When the lord of the tenth house is placed in the house of higher education, publications, knowledge, religion, and long-distance travel, the profession of the person is influenced by these qualities. They are highly educated people and keep upgrading their skills.

- They learn quickly and work hard to advance their career.
- They travel long distances for higher education.
- They take up jobs away from their birthplace.
- Their profession involves long-distance travel.
- They are very optimistic people and are interested in religious activities.
- They like to read religious scriptures and keep a collection of books.

8.5.10 10th Lord in the 10th House

When the lord of the 10th house is in the 10th house itself, the person sees a stable career in his life as the lord takes care of his own house. The nature of the profession of the person depends on the sign and the lord. Such a person does not have to struggle much in his career, he gets entry easily and sees steady progress. This is the house of rules and orders and the person works in senior positions in the organization where people follow his orders. A strong tenth house indicates that the person has a strong social status and gets respect and recognition for his work.

8.5.11 10th Lord in the 11th House

The 11th house is the house of income and desire, therefore a person's work, social status, career, and income are deeply intertwined with it and these people are highly inclined towards achieving all these things in life.

Career and income are their top priorities as they have many unfulfilled desires. They get support from their friends and siblings. They are good at networking, media, technology, and support the downtrodden in society, and prefer to work that has humanitarian benefits.

8.5.12 10th Lord in the 12th House

The 12th house represents foreign lands, hospitals, and debt repayment. When the 10th lord is placed in the 12th house, the person travels to foreign lands in connection with his work or his spouse's work. These people deal with debt repayment, hospitals, prisons, asylums, and suicide cases.

This house represents the secret workings of the human mind. Hence, it is the house of conspiracies, deceptions, and frauds and these people are either involved in such activities or have jobs in departments where the officials work in secret to catch the criminals. Its connection with secret matters indicates that these people can hide their work place, activities, affairs, matters related to their work from others for a long time. This is the house of isolation and dismissal from the job and a bad twelfth house indicates termination and isolation. These people work in a place far away from the city like a prison, airport, etc.

8.6 Upachaya House

The third, sixth, tenth and eleventh houses are called Upachaya House. The planets situated in Upachaya House help in the progress of a person. Therefore, the Mahadasha of these planets is very important. Among the body parts, the tenth house represents the knees. Just like knees help us to run and stand, similarly the planets situated in the tenth house help in the progress of a person.

Chapter 9

Profession Related to Nakshatras

Nakshatras play an important role in choosing a profession. The birth nakshatra reflects the inner nature and instinctive qualities of a person while the nakshatra of Lagna affects the body. However, a final decision cannot be taken based on just one factor as all the nakshatras and the related planets in the horoscope influence the individual. In this chapter, we will discuss about various professions related to all the 27 Nakshatras.

1. Ashwini: This nakshatra has a strong relation with travel, so, they do transport-related business. They do medicines and drug-related jobs and work as doctors, pediatricians, physiotherapists, and psychologists. They work in anything related to the beginning, as toy makers or sellers, children's books writers, kindergarten teachers, and tutors. They work as singers or any work related to voice and sound. They do work related to nurturing, counselors, social workers, and education-related work. They run fast, work as sports person and take participation in fun and adventurous sports.

2. Bharani: Doctors, Surgeons, Gynecologists, Midwives, IVF experts, and Pediatricians. They work for the entertainment & film industry, amusements, theme parks, play rounds, hospitality sectors like hotels and caterers, meat production, leather industry, construction, farming, and cosmetics. All activities connected with funerals and morgues, birth & death record-keeping officer, coffin makers, and obituary writer. They work for the tea, coffee, and tobacco industry. They work as geologists, and volcanic & earthquake experts. They are excellent at protecting someone, hence, they work as bodyguards.

3. Krittika: They work as heads of state or organizations, advisors, or administrative officers. They work for those jobs where cutting is involved, through a knife, blade, or some other sharp object. They work as surgeons, carpenters, butchers, barbers, tailors, blacksmiths, and chefs. They work for the weapon industry, military and police department, and electricity department. They work as a trainer, professor, spiritual teacher, discoverers, inventors, magicians, metaphysicians, and astronomers. They work for any work-related to fire, gold, furnace, and cooking. They do best for all those works where individual performance is considered and work as an entrepreneur.

4. Rohini: Banker, Accountant, Financial Advisor, Treasurer, Dancer, Musician, Singer, Fashion designer, Car designer, Model, Artist, Actor, Farmer, Cosmetics, Textiles, Environmentalist, and any work-related to agriculture, feeding, and creation.

5. Mrigashira: Mrigashira people prefer to work where movement is part of a profession. They don't like full day table jobs. They work as; Navigators, Explorers, Hunters, Writers, Salesman, Fashion designers, Farmers, Gardeners, Travel agents. They work for manufacturing and construction sector. Their eyes are always searching for some signal or their aim; hence, they work for defense sector. The ultimate search is for God, so they are Mystics.

6. Ardra: They work for investigation, analysis and jobs that require a high level of research work. They do better in psychology, pharmaceuticals, homeopathy, chemistry, biochemistry. They take a keen interest in storms and study weather and meteorology. They work for innovation and technology, computer science, electricity, photography, electronic music and weapon industry. They patiently wait for their time and work as a sniper.

7. Punarvasu: Such a person works for those jobs where success comes after multiple attempts, such as a job of computer programmer, sports, aerospace industry, medical research and development, and other testing jobs where multiple attempts are required to hit the target. They work as musicians where a person is able to play an instrument after several attempts.

They work with recycling industry and antique products. They work for construction industry, dam, bridges, roads etc. They work; travel & tourism industry, transport industry, Postal services, Communication, Newspaper and Media, Hotels, Delivery services, Travelers.

8. Pushya: Teaching, advisory and counselling services, investment planners, charity and non-profit organization workers, profession related with child care and nurturing, restaurant and hotels, dairy industry, music and art, personal secretary and hosts, priests and gurus, politicians and ministers, education department, volunteers and self-service persons, construction and water related work.

9. Ashlesha: Lawyer, politician, diplomat, reporter, journalist, and editor. They work for; the media and entertainment, paint industry, chemical, pharmaceuticals, pulp and paper, and plastics industries. They work in the medical field as scientists, chemists, pharmacists, and homeopaths.

10. Magha: Family business, Politics, Leader, Actor, TV hosts, Lawyers, Judges, Head, Musicians, Defense, Historians, Archeologists, Chartered Accountants, Investment consultants, Performers, Antique dealers, Entrepreneur, Public servant, Scientists, Professor, Construction related work, Hospitability, Genetics, Occultists, Astrologers, and any other work related to the study of past and requires deep roots for the future.

11. Purva Phalguni: Work related to film and entertainment, female products, fashion, cosmetics, beauticians, make-up artists, professional singers, and musicians. Work that requires delicate handling of products, decorations and event management, photography, etc.

12. Uttara Phalguni: These people have strong ability to show light and provide guidance to others. They work as Professor, Teacher, Trainer, Business advisor, Counselor, Sports-coach. They are good in research, discovery, astronomy and other jobs where findings are important after long search.

13. Hasta: These people work in those professions where dexterity of hand is required; Artists, Craftsmen, Painters, Performers, Writers, Comedians, and Dancers who use their hands in their arts. They work as; Stockbrokers, Bankers, Cleaners, Housekeepers, Gardeners, Farmers, Agriculturists, Typists. Such a person makes good shape of food and works with food production. They work as Barbers, Sculptors, Calligraphy, Tailors, and any job where the movement of fingers is important. They perform better in those sports where hands are important.

14. Chitra: Fashion designers, Jewellery designers, Cosmetic surgeons, Architects, Builders, Interior designers, City and Highway planners, Insurance agents,

Software designers, and Weapon Manufacturers. They love beauty and making things beautiful, so they work as; Embroiderers, Frame makers, Photographers, Make-up artists, and Cosmetologists. They love to design gadgets and work as Technicians, and Design engineers. They are business people and experts in their field. They can handle things with extreme care and work as: Midwives, Gynecologists, Pediatricians, Surgeons, Tailors, etc., and all those professions in which not a single wrong cut is allowed.

15. Swati: Pilots, Airhostess, Diplomats, Lawyers, Hosts, Musicians, Artists, PR professionals, Salesman, Yoga teacher, Aerobics and dance trainer, Diplomats, Entrepreneur, Businessmen, Experts in some field, Business of sound, Travel and tourism industry, Balloonists, Cleaning through vacuum cleaner, and any work where flow of air involves.

16. Vishakha: Lawyers, Entrepreneurs, Public Speakers, Professors, Priest, Preacher, Speech pathologists, Psychotherapist, Fashion models, Actresses, TV anchors, Broadcasters, Spokesperson, Mafia lords, Prostitutes, Revolutionists, Mountain climbers, Bartenders, Sportsperson, Soldiers, Guards. They like to do unusual professions and tough assignments.

17. Anuradha: These people are very good in those activities which require cooperation, like group activities of dancing, music, counselling, construction, travel agents, property brokers, factory workers, emergency related services, safety services, cleaning related services. Occultists, Numerologists, Statisticians and other activities which require understanding of high level of mathematical calculations. Agricultural activities, Team leaders, Surgeons, Mechanical Engineers, Damage control services, Patrolling services, and all other services which requires sideways movement in a group.

18. Jyeshtha: Politician, Leader, Philosopher, Corporate Executive, Chief, Head, Detective, Government Official, Military Leader, Entrepreneur, Sportsman, etc.

19. Mula: These people are suitable for research and investigation-related jobs. They work as medical surgeons, pharmacists, healers, and social workers. They are suitable for the legal profession, journalism, and politics. They work as the seller of Agri products, flowers, and fruits, etc. They take a deep interest in spirituality and work as a spiritual speaker and a priest. They quickly learn astrology, palmistry, and other occult science and advise others.

20. Purva Ashadha: Consultants, strategists, advisors, motivational speakers, research and investigation, and administrative jobs. They work as writers, editors, and all those jobs that require a high level of skill. They work for; Jobs related to filtration and air-related work, jobs that require debris removal, raw material processing, refinery, and product manufacturing where it is necessary to move raw materials through various processes to achieve a result. They deal with shipping and water utilities.

21. Uttara Ashadha: Finance, Teaching, Real estate, Military, Administration, Leader, Commander, Shooter, Bureaucrat, Entrepreneur, Social Worker, Scientific research, Priest, etc.

22. Shravana: They work as; professor, teacher, trainer, freelancers, preachers, researchers, storytellers, jugglers, magicians, musicians, anchors, actors, counselors, advisors, social workers, and performers. Planets in Sharavana indicate that such a person cannot work under anyone for long, they start their career as an employee but end it as an entrepreneur.

23. Dhanishta: Musician, drummer, artist, entertainer, choreographer, social worker, risk consultant, financial planners, insurance related professions, doctors, heart specialists, engineers, sports persons, coaches, administrators, managers, real estate persons, NGO workers, scientists, armed forces and police related professions.

24. Shatabhisha: Scientific jobs, Technological experts, Aeronautical science, Medicine and drugs, Physicians, Doctors, Surgeons. They are hunters, puzzle solvers and yoga experts. They take deep interest in psychology, astrology, and other healing techniques. They work for electricity and water department.

25. Purva Bhadrapada: Reformers, revolutionists, occultists, hermit, workers at crematorium and mortuary, official liquidator, trade settlers, scrap collector, surgeons and postmortem experts, weapon scientists and researchers, astrologers, palmists and esoteric practitioners, philosophers, teachers, trainers, psychoanalysts, politicians, encounter specialists, soldiers, speakers, work related with chemical and pharmaceutical industry, work related with demolition of buildings, work related with Insurance and Retirement planning. They work as journalists, TV anchors, news writers etc.

26. Uttara Bhadrapada: They are excellent in those jobs where a person has to write reports after research and findings. In financial market, they work as an analyst, who do research and write reports. They work as a news writer in media industry. They are eloquent speakers and they work as radio jockeys or TV anchors. This energy works for facial cleansing, Uttara Bhadrapada people often wash their face and like to apply make-up, women like to apply eyeliner (the same process of removing dust from water and in this case, surface is face).

They work for; Editing and Writing, Activity related to support someone, Research, Librarian, Work for humanitarian activities and for non-profit organizations, Charity organizations, Professor, Psychologist, Healers, Counselors, Waste Management, Cleaning something with water like Car cleaners, Floor cleaners, Make-up professionals, Watering related activities, Irrigation, Drainage, Fertilization activities. Profession related to catharsis, yoga and meditation. This energy says that the time is coming to leave everything; hence, they work as Insurance and retirement solution providers.

27. Revati: Traveller, Publisher, Editor, Journalist, Flight Attendant, Actor, Film Director, Artist, Musician, PR Personal, Comedian, Fiction Writer, Maintenance Personal, Magician, Hypnotist, Doctor, Surgeon, Teacher, Nurse, Baby Care, Customer Care.

Chapter 10

Ashtakvarga in Career

Ashtakvarga is a unique system in astrology to understand the strength and the result of transit of planets of each house. It is necessary to understand the point-based system and before reaching any conclusion observe the point obtained by each house in the native's chart. The growth of career and downfall depends upon the point obtained by the respective house.

Higher the numbers indicate significant growth and lower the number indicates problem. When these houses activate in transit the outcome also affects. In this chapter we will discuss about how this unique system affects the life of the person.

10.1 Basic Concept

'Ashta' means eight, and 'Varga' means classification, hence, the word Ashtakvarga means eight types of classifications. The classification is a combination of seven planets and lagna, these combinations create eight different types of energies which can be benefic or malefic and depend on the position of the planets. Maharishi Parashara introduced this concept in his book 'Brihat Parashara Hora Shastra' and it is a unique system of prediction in Hindu Astrology without which prediction is totally impossible.

There are total nine planets considered in Hindu Astrology, but the Ashtakvarga system considers only seven planets and leaves Rahu and Ketu, with lagna there are eight in number. Therefore, there are eight types of energies that every planet release and these can be good or bad. The release of benefic energy is called 'Bindus' (Dots) and the release of malefic energy is called 'Rekhas' (Small lines).

Preparing an Ashtakvarga table is beyond the scope of this book, but it is necessary to observe the points in each house before arriving at any conclusions as it provides many important information.

10.2 Interpretation of Ashtakvarga Table

In the table, we need to observe the total number of bindus obtained by the planet and the total bindus in the sign. The maximum number of bindus in a sign is 8, if a planet has 4 bindus then the result would be mediocre to good, more than 5 to 8 is very good to excellent.

Sun: On the scale of 8 bindus, the transit of the Sun would be considered strong if it obtained more than 5 binus in a sign. An excellent result would be possible when more bindus is obtained, 4 is considered as average, and less than 4 means inauspicious results likely to be possible.

Moon: If bindus are 5 or more then the transit bestows the person with favourable results, 4 is considered average, 1 to 3 indicates pessimism are 0 means melancholic state of mind.

Mars: Up to 3 bindus, Mars is considered weak and leads to quarrels, pessimism, loss of status and wealth. 4 bindus gives average results while 5 to 8 bindus are excellent.

Mercury: 4 bindus are average, 5 to 8 are excellent and 0 to 3 are poor. Weak Mercury in 6th or 8th houses with poor bindus - the person becomes unreliable and crooked in behavior.

Jupiter: 4 bindus are average, 5 to 8 are excellent, success, gain of wealth, and 0 to 3 are poor. A weak Jupiter with poor bindus, life will become unfortunate and full of struggles.

Venus: 4 bindus are average, 5 to 8 are excellent and 0 to 3 are poor. Weak Venus causes marital problems, poverty, scandals, and life without meaning.

Saturn: 4 bindus are average, 5 to 8 are excellent and 0 to 3 are poor. Weak Saturn causes hindrances, delays, sickness, death, disease, and poverty.

10.3 Sarvashtakvarga

The total points in the Sarvashtakvarga table are 337. These points are divided into 12 bhavas, divide 337 into 12, 28 is the average point for each bhava. However, the minimum number of points is different for each bhava, but 28 is considered as strong. If a bhava has more than 28 points then it is considered a strong bhava and able to generate auspicious results. As the numbers are higher the result would be much better, transit of planets over these bhavas able to produce favourable results. The points below 28 are considered as weak bhava, if the count falls below 21 then it is inauspicious, a lower number means to struggle and problems and transit of the planet may produce adverse results.

The minimum number of bindus for each bhava is:

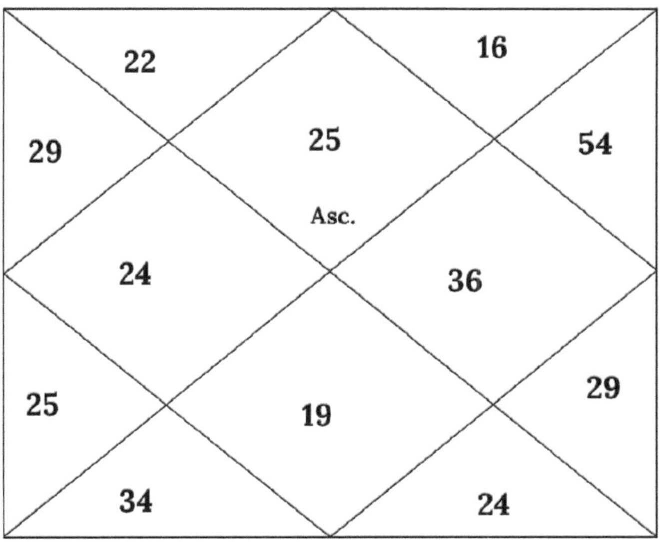

Lagna - Lagna represents the self, the points in this bhava indicate the confidence of the person. The points here more than 28 indicate the courageous nature of the person, such type of person does not feel panic in adverse circumstances. Less than 25 points indicate a lack of courage and less than 21 points means coward person.

2nd House - More points in the second house indicate enough savings for the person.

3rd House - It is the house of courage; more points indicate brave nature while fewer points indicate dependency and lack of initiative.

4th House - It is the house of home, comfort, and early education. Points in this house more than 24 indicate smooth education, and comfort at home, while fewer points indicate problems in education and lack of resources.

5th House - It is the house of creation, interest, and children. Fewer points mean difficulty in getting children, the person faces extreme difficulties to fulfill his dreams.

6th House - This is the house of immunity. More points indicate strong immunity of the person, while fewer points mean easily vulnerable to diseases.

7th House - This is the house of spouse and partnership. More points mean good relations with spouse, if points are below 15 indicates a problem with spouse and partners.

8th House - This is the house of longevity. Fewer points do not mean less longevity but a depressed state of mind where a person lacks the necessary vitality and vigour in his life.

9th House - This is the house of religion and higher education. Fewer points indicate the person has no belief in religion and may face problems in getting higher education.

10th House - More points indicate the person is responsible for his duties while fewer points indicate careless nature.

11th House - More points indicate higher income with less work, while fewer points indicate struggle in getting income.

12th House - This is the house of expenditure, so fewer points are good, more points indicate a spendthrift person. Very less points mean a miser person.

10.4 Ashtakvarga Analysis

While analyzing the Ashtakvarga table, it is necessary to check the numbers of each planet along with the numbers obtained from each house. The transit of Jupiter and Saturn plays an important role in a person's life. Therefore, their high or low numbers in a house give important results. If the time is favorable but the numbers in the Ashtakvarga table are low, then only minor gains are obtained in career and low numbers indicate trouble.

It is necessary to examine the points obtained in the 10th and the 11th house. The yardstick to check the points is given in the table above. However, for a strong career both of the house's points should be more than 28. If the house of income (11th) has more points than the house of karma (10th) then the person will see an increase in income through his efforts.

More points indicate that the source of income is good. If the house of karma (10th) has more points than the house of income (11th) then the person will have to work hard to increase his income and success in life will not come easily.

More difference of points between the two houses indicates stagnation in career. Such a person works hard for his growth but there comes a time in his life when it seems as if his career is stuck at the same place for a long time.

Low points in one house should not be considered bad if the other house has high points. It indicates that career is not easy and one needs to work hard for it because despite a weak house, a strong second house has the potential to take a person's career forward.

Chapter 11

Downfall in Career

Changes are inevitable in life and every step taken by a person is not always pleasant. People take a path only when they think it is good and they are going to be successful, but the results are not always as expected. Some people struggle a lot to get their first success, they knock many doors to get their first job and some get success easily. Some people get success in the first half of their life and face downfall in the second half. While some people's careers shine in their second half, the first half of their career is full of struggle.

Situations in life keep changing like day turns into night and night into day. But people think that what is going on will continue forever. If they are going through a phase of good days then they think that it will continue forever and never think that there can be a reversal in their life. Similarly, when people are going through a phase of bad days in their life then they start feeling that this nightmare will never end. Their efforts will never succeed and after making a few efforts they stop and start blaming their fate.

I have learned that the hard work done by a person never goes in vain. You may not get the fruits of your hard work when you expect it, but whatever work you have done, you will definitely get the fruits of it one day. The person who works hard to get results has a strong Saturn and the person who wants to get results without working hard has a strong Rahu. Therefore, Saturn represents pressure and hard work and Rahu represents greed.

In this chapter we will discuss various astrological causes for conflict, stress, job change, profession change and downfall in professional life.

11.1 Saturn - The Tough Master

Saturn is the sixth planet from the Sun and the second-largest planet in our solar system. Saturn is a very powerful planet and its effect on life is subtle and more than any other planet, but its effect is very slow and not easily visible. Only those who have the quality of patience can see the effect of Saturn. It controls our muscles, hair, and nails. Our muscles change, but we don't know when; Our hair and nails grow and we don't know when they grew, this is how the energy of Saturn works - gradually and very slowly.

Saturn is considered as "Tough Master" and teaches hard work and patience in life. On the path of Ultimate Truth, it requires immense patience, therefore, those who do not have patience and want everything fast and without any effort then Saturn teaches them a tough lesson. Therefore, position of Saturn in a horoscope is very important to consider.

A seed cannot become a tree without enduring pressure. It is a process of transformation in which the identity of the seed is completely lost and a huge tree grows in its place.

Saturn changes a person completely and the lessons taught by Saturn are remembered by the person throughout his life. When Saturn starts putting pressure on life, the favorable wind becomes unfavorable, work starts to stop and success becomes difficult. Troubles start and it seems that everything in life has frozen. The pressure given by Saturn is a part of change and that change is permanent in a person's life.

Saturn in Ascendant: When Saturn situated in ascendant its 10th aspect is on 10th house. Any influence on Saturn to the 10th house indicates that the professional life of the person may not go smoothly. The tough master teaches necessary lessons to the person and for this the person has to go through difficult phases in life. There is a deep meaning behind every obstacle and Saturn forces the person to remove whatever is unnecessary in life.

Saturn in 4th house: When Saturn is placed in the fourth house, its seventh aspect is on the tenth house. Such a person has to face many types of struggles in life and matters related to home and workplace are always stressful. Saturn is considered the planet of justice and the order given by the judge has to be followed, there is no meaning of liking or disliking in this, otherwise force can also be used to fulfill the order. Similarly, Saturn teaches a tough lesson to the person forcefully and the more ego there is, the more pain there will be.

Saturn in the 8th House: When Saturn is placed in the eighth house, its third aspect is on the tenth house. Such a person has to face many difficulties in life to complete his work. A mountain of difficulties may stand in front of the person, but the positive thing is that the person has the power to face all these difficulties.

Saturn placed in the eighth house gives a long life to the person and the person has to go through many challenges and emerges as a winner by crossing all the obstacles one by one. Big challenges give birth to great personalities.

Saturn in the 10th House: The tenth house is Saturn's own house where the planet gives good results, but such a person succeeds only after much hard work. Such a person never shies away from working hard and can occupy high positions in life.

Saturn in the tenth house indicates that one day the person will open his venture but first, he will have to struggle for a job. The struggle given by Saturn is not to block the career but to learn new skills, later his struggle and experience help him to succeed. (Note: This topic already discussed in chapter 8.)

11.2 Sun – Saturn Conjunction

Sun is the soul which represents light and Saturn is the main ruler of death and represents darkness. These are two opposite energies. According to astrology, the relationship between Sun and Saturn is inimical. When planets with opposite energies meet in any house of the horoscope then they do not support each other and start dominating to show their supremacy and this creates disturbance in the matter of that house. For example, Sun is the indicator of time and Saturn is the indicator of the end of time.

Hence, this combination shows that the watch of such a person will never work properly, either he will lose it or it will get damaged. The poor watch has been gone in the fight between Sun and Saturn. There is another meaning of this conjunction. Damage of watch indicates damage of time, the Sun-Saturn conjunction indicates a delay in time. Therefore, there is a delay in things happening and nothing happens on time in their lives.

Following are some more differences for better understanding of these two energies;

1. Sun is a fiery planet, due to its influence things become hot, active and agile. Saturn is a cold planet, due to its influence things become freeze and isolated, speed slows down and every activity stops.

2. Sun is the king and Saturn is the guard. When the king arrives, the doors are opened and the guard's job is to close and lock the doors. When the Sun comes in the morning the darkness goes away, when the Sun goes in the evening the darkness returns. One energy forces the door to open and the other energy forces the door to close. These two are opposite functions and both cannot happen simultaneously.

3. Sun is the beginning of activity and Saturn brings limits, restrictions and takes things to their end; Saturn is "The End".

4. Sun represents autocracy and Saturn represents democracy.

5. Sun shows ego and Saturn brings down every ego. Saturn shows the real truth of life and makes the person humble by removing all types of ego.

6. There is always a conflict between the Sun and Saturn when they are together or opposite each other, and this conflict intensifies during the transit.

Hence, this combination indicates overcoming ego because Saturn means being devoid of ego. Saturn creates many obstacles to reduce the ego, this shows that the more ego a person has, the more obstacles he will have to face in his life. Saturn is an emotionless planet which teaches discipline and hard work in life. This combination makes the person extremely practical who stays away from all kinds of gossip and manipulation.

Rahu work as an agent to Saturn and has full power to engulf the Sun i.e., remove light in the life of the person. Therefore, giving up ego and becoming a humble person is the only key to overcome the negative effects of this conjunction. If this conjunction occurs in Aries then it indicates a high ego whereas if it occurs in Libra then it indicates a humble person.

Sun represents father and authority and Saturn who is his son represents masses and working-class people. Saturn is the planet of justice and brings balance. The judge shows no mercy while giving justice. That is why Saturn shows no mercy to the Sun and destroys all its negativity. This combination indicates that the person will not have a cordial relationship with his bosses and will challenge his superiors for any wrong doing. It indicates wild arguments between father or authority figure and in transit the situation become worst. Therefore, the career of these individuals is inconsistent as both Sun and Saturn are the karakas of the tenth house which is the house of career and the fight between these two, spoils the career like a watch gone haywire in the above example.

In the house in which this conjunction occurs, the person has to face various obstacles. For example, if this conjunction falls in the fifth house then the person faces problems in his creativity and the child is our creation. Therefore, such a person has to face problems in marital life or problems related to children or he works very hard and his creation gets destroyed without any reason.

If this combination comes in the fourth or tenth house, then it is not good for his professional life. He has to face a lot of struggle to make his way. The aspect of these two planets with each other in the fourth and tenth houses also creates a lot of struggle in the native's professional life and he gets initial success in his career after a lot of struggle. The maturity age of Sun is 22 years and the maturity age of Saturn is 36 years. Hence, the life of such a person between the age of 22 to 36 years is full of struggle.

On the Downside: The downside is that they become undisciplined and pessimistic individuals who lack goals in life. Instead of becoming humble, they become timid, avoid challenges and do not have the courage to face adversities.

The Positive Thing: The positive thing is that this combination gives birth to a very mature person. However, many kinds of obstacles come in their life but they are always ready to fight them. They tend to be self-made individuals and achieve success through their own efforts, although their learning curve may be longer than others. They become down to earth people and are ready to remove darkness from life. They remain isolated from others, become spiritual and take interest in occult.

On the higher aspect, this combination indicates that the person will seek the light but will have to go on the path of darkness and one cannot move towards the light without seeing the real truth of life where the biggest obstacle is one's ego.

11.3 Jupiter in Capricorn

Capricorn is the 10th sign of the zodiac and is ruled by Saturn. Jupiter gets debilitated in this sign at 5 degrees. This earthy sign keeps everything in full control. The planet of expansion feels highly misfit in this sign because Capricorn puts control and restrictions on everything and does not allow Jupiter to move. We can say that the sky is under control in Capricorn.

Therefore, after entering this sign Jupiter feels highly uncomfortable and gets debilitated. It means such a person has to face the lack of resources in his life, he has a great desire for expansion but he moves only inch by inch.

Due to the effect of Saturn, these people don't like to mingle with people and prefer aloofness in life. The presence of Jupiter indicates morality and discipline are at the highest level. Jupiter and Saturn are neutral towards each other. Discipline is required in the path of spirituality so that a person can easily follow such a path in life.

Capricorn is represented by the sea-goat, a mythological creature with the body of a goat and the tail of a fish. The first half of the sign is quadruped and the second half is footless. The first 15 degrees are non-movable and the second 15 degrees have a tail which signifies movement. When Jupiter is placed in the first 15 degrees of the sign, then such a person faces too many restrictions in his life. It makes a person a strict ideologist who is not ready to compromise under any circumstances. Once they decide, then it is very difficult to change it.

When Jupiter is in the second half of Capricorn, movement is witnessed, and activity increases. Such a person listens to the advice of others and makes decisions as per the circumstances. They always discuss rationally. Their approach is very practical and very good at planning. Jupiter means wisdom, so they are not satisfied with superficial observation but prefer to delve deeper into the matter. Capricorn means uses at the highest level. Although the resources are limited, they have a strong ability to overcome all the difficulties.

Gold drives the world economy and Jupiter represents gold. In ancient times, gold was the medium of buying and selling. Therefore, gold represents the income of a person. For wealth strong Jupiter is required in a horoscope. Weak and afflicted Jupiter in D1 and D9 chart indicates financial problems in life.

11.4 Transit of Saturn Over Jupiter in Capricorn

When Saturn transits in Capricorn, the income of people who have Jupiter in Capricorn in their horoscope suddenly stops for 2.5 years and during that time the activities of such a person become very limited. The circumstances make a person immobile and it seems as if everything has frozen.

Example: Suppose the ascendant in someone's horoscope is Sagittarius. The second house is Capricorn and the natal Jupiter is placed in this house. When Saturn enters Capricorn in transit, financial problems start in the person's life. His earnings will stop for 2.5 years and his savings will start running out.

The Story of the Elephant and the Crocodile: Remember the kid's story of "An Elephant and a Crocodile." There was a very powerful elephant. Once he went to the river to drink water. A very powerful crocodile lived in that river. He caught the elephant's leg and started pulling it into the deep water. Both were equally strong, but the crocodile's strength in the water was more than that of the elephant.

The elephant tried his best to free himself from the crocodile's mouth but his efforts were not successful. Then the elephant called Lord Vishnu for help. The Lord cut off the crocodile's head with his Surdarshan Chakra and freed the elephant.

Jupiter is represented by an elephant and Saturn by a crocodile. The above story is a symbolic representation of the situation that occurs when Jupiter is placed in Capricorn and Saturn transits over it. These ancient stories have a lot of importance and these stories tell about the deeper meaning of life.

Saturn entered Capricorn on 23rd January 2020: I observed that people who are above 36 years of age and have Jupiter placed in Capricorn in their horoscope lost their active source of income during that period. People who were doing service suffered from job loss and those who are doing business suffered from various kinds of troubles. This was the phase of transition and this transit changed the lives of all those people who had Jupiter in Capricorn. However, during that time, there was an epidemic all over the world and people were paralyzed.

It is said that Saturn shows people the real world. When the source of income stopped, these people saw the real face of their friends and colleagues, which they would not have known if such a phase had not come in their life. So, it is true that transit of Saturn shows the real world to a person and it clears all the cover from the face.

11.5 Saturn's Dasha, Venus Antardasha

When we explore such a period in ancient text, Chapter XII, first stanza of Bhavartha Ratnakar states that "When Saturn's dasha, Venus bhukti starts or Venus dasha Saturn bhukti begins, such period is highly unfortunate for the person." Venus is the planet of luxury and comfort and Saturn hates all these things.

Saturn is the planet which keeps the person secluded and devoid of all kinds of luxuries and comforts. Saturn teaches hard lesson to the person and shows the harsh truth of life which a person cannot see in his heydays.

Such period lasts for a person for 3 years and 2 months. I have seen that such period is extremely troublesome for those people whose Saturn's dasha, Venus bhukti face when they are at the heydays of their career.

During this period 'The Tough Master' teaches tough lessons to the person and the person remember such lessons during their whole life.

11.6 Mercury-Rahu Conjunction

Mercury-Rahu conjunction indicates a disruption in income for some time. Rahu is the planet of sudden events and can cause sudden gains or losses. Mercury is considered an important planet for business including communication, finance, and management. This conjunction indicates a temporary disruption in business or a decrease in income or no income for some time followed by a sudden increase in income.

The problem in income is activated due to dasha or transit and its duration may be till the duration of the respective dasha or transit. Disruption in the regular flow of income starts creating problems in life, and these problems can persist for a few years. The positive side is that such situations force the person to think differently. Life provides them with an opportunity to hone their skills. When the period of disruption ends, they come out as a very experienced and mature person, and suddenly their income increases.

11.7 Grahan Dosha

Grahan dosh takes place due to Rahu, Ketu, Sun, and Moon. When the Sun or Moon is placed with Rahu or Ketu in a chart, then Grahan Dosh happens.

If such a Grahan Dosha is present on the fourth or tenth house in the horoscope, it is not good for the professional career of the native and the person may face many difficulties at a certain time. I have observed that the Sun-Rahu conjunction in these houses is not good for a stable career. Such a native often faces job changes or relocations.

Rahu is a turbulent energy and has full power to swallow the Sun at the time of eclipse. Therefore, the sunlight disappears at the time of solar eclipse and the native faces problems related to his home and workplace. The maturity age of Rahu is 42 years; therefore, not every solar eclipse is bad, we have to consider in which nakshatra the eclipse is taking place and the age of the person.

If Sun is the lord of Dusthana Bhava (6th, 8th and 12th) and is placed in the fourth or tenth house along with Rahu, then such a person faces a setback in life after 42 years at the time of solar eclipse. If during this time Rahu is transiting in Leo and there is a solar eclipse, then such a problem in life persists for 1.5 years because Rahu stays in one sign for 1.5 years.

11.8 Vipreet Raj Yoga

This yoga is formed when planets ruling a dusthana house (6,8,12) occupy another dusthana.

- Harsha yoga–The 6th lord is in the 8th or the 12th house
- Sarala yoga-The 8th lord is in the 6th or 12th
- Vimala yoga–The 12th lord is in the 6th or 8th

It is said to give sudden unexpected rise in life, usually after an initial setback or misfortune.

When the lords of the 6th, 8th, and 12th houses are inimical planets and they are placed in the 4th and 10th houses then such a combination creates a lot of hindrance in the professional career of the native in the initial stage of his life.

For example, Sun and Saturn are considered enemy planets and if both these planets are the lords of the Dusthana Bhava and are placed opposite to each other in the fourth and tenth houses then the native gets his first job after a lot of struggle. In this position, the Sun and Saturn are 180 degrees away from each other and Saturn is also retrograde.

Retrograde Saturn is more powerful and the Sun becomes weak. Due to the influence of opposite energies, such a person progresses slowly in his career and has to face struggle at every stage. There will be progress in his life but only after a setback.

Vipreet Raj Yoga: From Lack of Resources to Plenty of Resources

When a period of failure begins, the person loses his source of income and starts getting upset with his profession. But Vipreet Raj Yoga means that after some time he will start his career again. Suddenly he will get a job or do well in business, even if there is a period of long break present in his biodata. After a gap, a new source of income suddenly opens up. His talent starts getting respected and the path to move forward in life starts appearing.

Raj Yoga means an abundance of resources. Vipreet means opposite, against, or not being supportive. In other words, we can say that there is no support or the circumstances are unfavorable. Vipreet Raj Yoga means that resources will be available but first, the person has to see the completely opposite circumstances in life i.e. lack of resources. If Vipreet Raj Yoga is present then the person has to face adversity first in life. He has to struggle a lot to complete even a simple task.

The pace of development in life is languid and there is a time when he does not see any support and no one is ready to help, but at the 11th hour, the person is saved, and then his career starts moving forward.

The process of resurrection begins in life. So, if Vipreet Raj Yoga is present, then such a person has to face misfortune first and after that Raj Yoga is completed in his life.

We can understand this process from the germination of seed. Seed dormancy is the state where the seed will not germinate, even under ideal conditions, unless the protective barriers are broken. Many seeds have developed these protective barriers to tolerate adverse conditions and to avoid being destroyed by dangerous weather.

Seed dormancy helps the plant survive, but sometimes it becomes a hindrance to those who want to grow plants from seed at home. This state of the seed can be broken by temperature, moisture, and light. Germination requires that this dormant state be broken. When the seed coat is hard it requires more pressure than a normal seed to germinate.

When everything is easily available, learning stops and the mind goes into a dormant state. Vipreet Raj Yoga is like breaking the tough seed coat for germination. Various adverse circumstances in life create pressure to grow which might not have happened if the person had the resources. After enduring the pressure, his hidden talent has come to the fore and now he is ready to become a big tree.

11.9 Kartari Yoga

- **Shubh Kartari Yoga - Good Neighbours**

- **Paap Kartari Yoga - Bad Neighbours**

Shubh Kartari Yoga is formed when a planet or a house is surrounded by benefic planets from both its sides and Paap Kartari Yoga is formed when a planet or a house is surrounded by malefic planets on both sides without any beneficial aspect.

This yoga can be understood better with a situation when both of the neighbours are good then they will help and when both of the neighbours are bad then no help will come. They will affect the house and create unnecessary problems. Shubh kartari yoga increases the auspiciousness of the planet or house while Paap Kartari yoga tends to cause difficulty for that planet or house.

Example: If Jupiter is situated in the 11th house and Venus is situated in the 9th house then it is considered as Shubh Kartari Yoga. This is an auspicious yoga because both the neighbours of the 10th house is good and they provide their every support and tend to promote the activities at the work place. But suppose if in these two houses Saturn and Rahu are situated then they hamper the growth of the 10th house, such a person faces various obstacles in his career and when one problem has gone then another is waiting for them.

For the growth of the professional life it is important to consider the Kartari yoga related with the 10th house.

11.10 The Rahu - Ketu Axis

When these nodes are placed in the 4th and the 10th houses in the horoscope, the matters related to these houses are not stable. Rahu in the 10th house means that there is always instability in the professional life and the situation becomes even worse if Rahu is placed with enemy planets. The career of such a person is unstable and it is not possible for them to stay in one place for a long time, as this energy always keeps creating some or the other disturbances.

So, they move from one job to another, one company to another, one business to another. After 18 years, when Rahu transits over the natal Rahu, such disturbances increase and it lasts for 1.5 years.

Ketu in the 10th house means sudden separation from the work place, it also indicates job loss or the person leaving his job voluntarily. Ketu has no attachment to the place where it is placed, so Ketu in the 10th house means that such a person has no attachment to his job. He is more interested in finding secrets and research related activities. These people do not like to blow the trumpet of their work and do not like to show their face to others. These are aloof people who are happy with the discovery of things that are not easily visible. The transit of Ketu in the 10th house brings significant changes in the professional life of a person.

The Rahu-Ketu axis shows our karmic connections from our past lives - what we did and what we want to achieve. This axis of the fourth and tenth house shows that changes related to their professional life are inevitable in their lives.

11.11 Termination or Job Loss

People are afraid of losing their jobs and try every possible way to save them. But many people face such a problem in their lives. After one job, some people get another job quickly, but some people take time. They do not know when they will get the next job or when their next career will start, and as time passes, they get frustrated. Astrology helps identify the chances of service termination and when the person will get the next opportunity.

Houses of Termination, Job Loss, or Suspension: The 12th house from any house is its negator. Following are the houses when activated simultaneously and connected then such a person has to face problems related to their work and professional life.

1st House: It is the negator of the 2nd house. The 2nd house represents savings, possessions, acquisitions, and finances. It is the house of self-acquisition.

5th house: It is the negator of the 6th house. The 6th house represents our daily activities, service, and employment.

8th house: It is the house of transformation, misery and unexpected events in life.

9th house: It is a negator of the 10th house. The 10th house represents profession, source of livelihood, and status.

12th house: It is the house of loss and expenditure and the negator of the 11th house.

When all these houses are active at a certain time then the person has to leave his job or profession and till these houses are active it is possible that he may not get a second option.

Next Opportunity: When the earth houses (2nd, 6th, and 10th) are active then the person will start his next job or profession. The eleventh house is the house of profit, when this house is also active along with the earthy houses then the native's career shines. When all four houses are strong and active in Dasha or transit then the native gets much success in his efforts.

Conclusion

Astrology helps us to recognize our qualities and talents and channelize the energy in a proper way so that we can move in the right direction. One should stay away from external influences and move ahead in life by recognizing his inner talent.

When the planetary energies force one to halt the activities of the outer world, such time should be used to develop skills. Every event in life happens with a purpose. Therefore, wise people use such time to sow seeds, so that they can achieve success when the time is favorable.

Downfall does not mean the end of the career. There is no straight move in the world and everything moves in a circle. The cycle of day and night is the law of nature. A true human being is one who can stay away from stress and face the storm. Those who face the storm and keep trying to achieve their goal through hard work find new ways in life. There is no stopping in the continuous flow of the universe, it goes on uninterrupted, and that is why life never stops anywhere.

Chapter 12

Illustrations

Example 1: Police Department Employee

D1 Chart

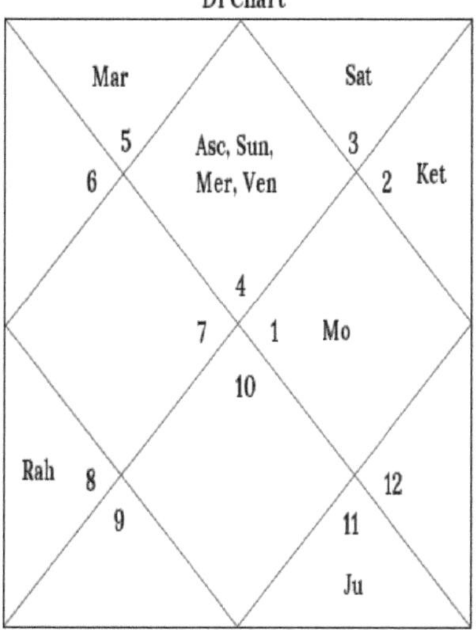

D10 Chart

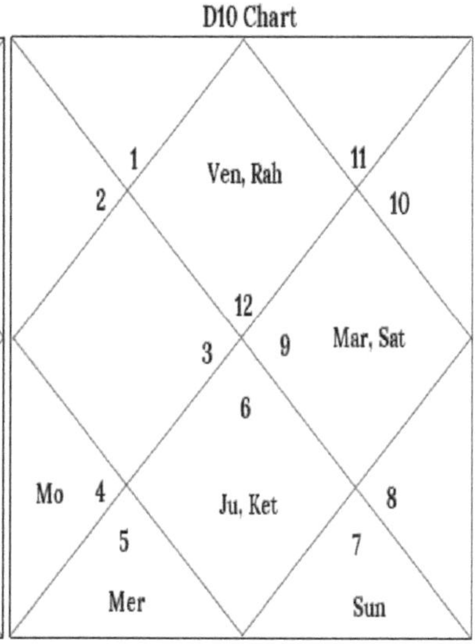

1. In the D1 chart, the 10th house from the Lagna and Sun is Aries. The lord of Aries is Mars which is placed in Leo in the 2nd house.

2. In the D10 chart, Mars is placed in Sagittarius with Saturn in the 10th house.

3. In D1 chart, Moon in the 10th house indicates receiving orders and following them.

4. Mars pulled the person to the police department, where the native gets transferred to deal with legal matters due to the influence of Saturn.

5. In the D1 chart, the lord of the 6th house is Jupiter which is placed in the 8th house which indicates investigation and probing activities.

6. In the D10 chart, Mercury is placed in the 6th house in Leo which indicates the intelligence involved in his work.

7. In the D1 chart, the lord of the Lagna is Moon and in the D10 chart the lord of the Lagna is Jupiter. Jupiter and Moon are friends of each other. The person got the job easily without any struggle in his life.

8. In D10 chart, Jupiter and Ketu in the 7th house indicate that one day the person will start his own venture, which will happen to him when the dasha of that planet comes.

Example 2: Sales and Marketing Professional

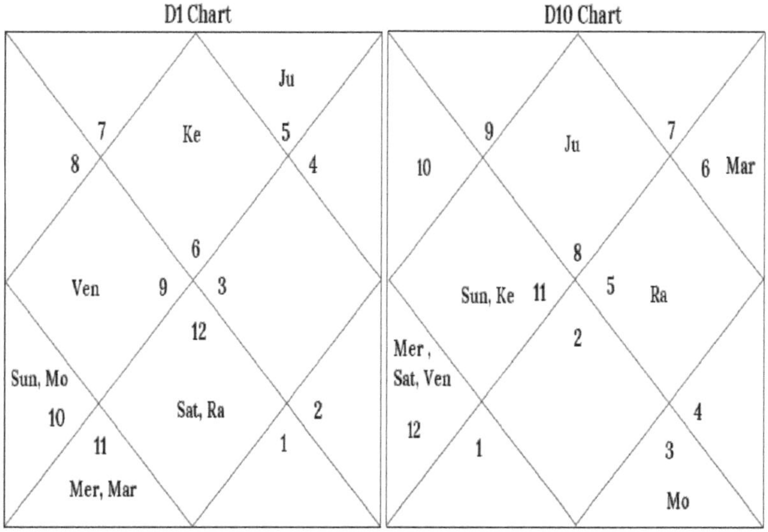

1. In D1 chart, 10th house from Lagna is Gemini whose lord is Mercury and it is placed in 6th house with Mars. 10th house from Sun and Moon is Libra whose lord is Venus placed in 4th house.

2. In D10 chart, there is no planet in 6th and 7th house, and Rahu is placed in 10th house. We have to check the position and strength of its lord in D1 chart.

3. In D10 chart, 6th lord is Mars which is placed in 6th house in D1 chart which is Aquarius sign ruled by Saturn and Jupiter has 7th aspect on it. The 7th lord is Venus which is placed in 4th house in Jupiter sign.

4. So, the planets influencing the native's profession are - Mars, Mercury, Rahu and Venus.

5. Mars, the fiery planet indicates energy involve in his daily activities with intelligence of Mercury. Rahu indicates that the person is desirous and achieving goal is important for him no matter by what means.

6. Influence of Venus indicates a neat and clean atmosphere, proper keeping of documents at its place and fine tuning.

7. The 8th lord Mars in the 6th house indicates that the matter of loans and debt involve in his daily activities.

Example 3: Bank Officer

D1 Chart

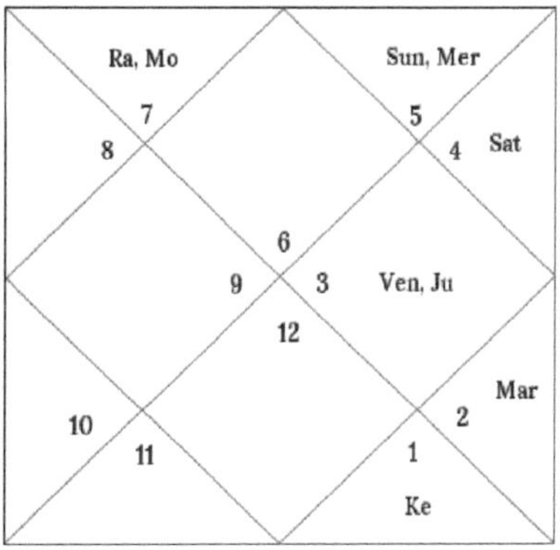

D10 Chart

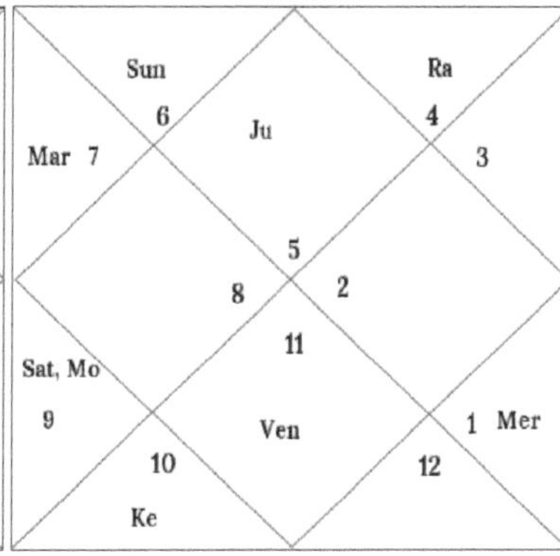

1. In the D1 chart, the 10th house from the Lagna is Gemini where Jupiter and Venus are placed. The presence of Jupiter in the 10th house indicates ease in getting a job.

2. Sun and Mercury placed in the 12th house are aspecting the 6th house while there is no aspect on the 7th house.

3. Jupiter's 9th aspect is also on the 6th house, which makes the 6th house strong. 4. In the D1 chart, the Lagna lord is Mercury and in the D10 chart the Lagna lord is Sun and both are friends.

5. Due to the presence of Jupiter in the 10th house and Mercury aspecting the 6th house, the person got selected easily in the bank officer exam and is currently working in a PSU bank.

Example 4: Private Sector Employee

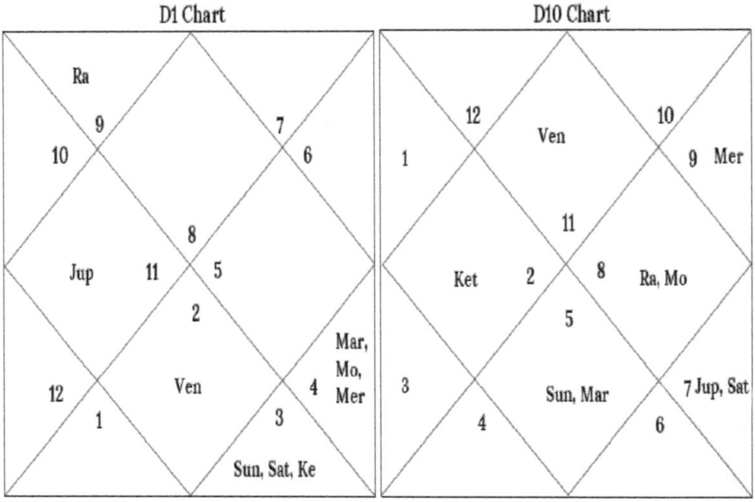

1. In D1 chart, the 10th house is Leo sign ruled by Sun which is placed in the 8th house, the house of transformation.

2. The 6th house is ruled by Mars which is debilitated in the 9th house and the 7th house is ruled by Venus which is there.

3. Jupiter in the 4th house is aspecting the 10th house which indicates ease in getting a job and security at the workplace. The person faced many critical situations in life like the possibility of losing his job and office politics, but every time he is protected.

4. The Sun-Saturn conjunction in the 8th house in D1 chart indicates struggle in career but is protected by Jupiter in the 4th house.

5. In D10 chart, two planets Sun and Mars are in the 7th house which makes his business outlook strong and is also supported by Mercury in the 11th house.

6. The person had a great desire to open his own venture, but circumstances did not allow him to do so.

7. When he reached middle age, he lost his job. The placement of Sun, the lord of the 10th house, in the 8th house, indicates transformation is inevitable in his life.

8. His destiny forces him to open his own venture, which is reflected in the 7th house in the D10 chart.

Example 5: Business Man

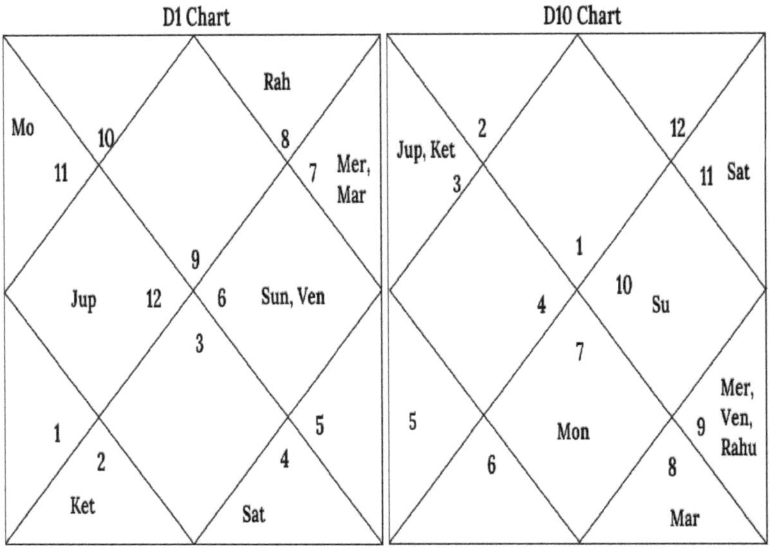

1. In D1 chart, the 10th house is Virgo sign ruled by Mercury and placed in 11th house, which is the house of gains.

2. Sun placed in 10th house is the lord of 9th house and Venus also placed in 10th house which is the lord of 11th and 6th house.

3. 10th house from Moon is 12th house where Rahu is placed and indicates foreign relations. Rahu-Ketu indicate activities related to import-export.

4. 10th house from Sun is 7th house ruled by Mercury and placed in 11th house.

5. 7th aspect of Jupiter in 10th house indicates ease in workplace.

6. Saturn in 8th house indicates difficulties in saving as it is the lord of 2nd house but also the lord of 3rd house which indicates entrepreneurship.

7. In D10 chart, Moon is placed in the 7th house and Mars in the 8th house.

8. All the above combinations indicate that the person will do business and run his venture successfully.

Bibliography

Brihat Parashara Hora Sastra by Maharshi Parasara

Brihat Jatak, Translation by Prof. P.S. Sastri, Rajan Publications, New Delhi

Jatak Parijat, Translation by V. Subramanya Sastri, Rajan Publications, New Delhi

Hora Sara, by Prithuyasas (Translation by R. Santhanam)

Scientific Hindu Astrology Vol 1 &2 by P.S. Sastri

Phaladeepika, by Mantreshwar's (Translation by V. Subrahmanya Sastri)

Hindu Science of the Future by Harihar Majumder

Sarvarth Chintamani by Vyankatesh Sharma (Translation by J.N. Bhasin)

Studies in Jaimini Astrology, Translation by B.V. Raman, MLBD, Delhi

Jaimini Sutram, Translation by Prof. P.S. Sastri, Rajan Publications, New Delhi

Varga Charka, Sagar Publications, New Delhi

Saravali Vol 1 &2 (Translation by R. Santhanam)

Fundamental Principals of Astrology by Prof. KS. Krishnamurti

Predictive Steller Astrology by Prof. KS. Krishnamurti

Techniques of Predicting Future by Dr. Nimai Banerjee, Bhagyalipi Publications, Cuttack

Planetary Behavior & Human Life, Bhagyalipi Publications, Cuttack

Navamsa-lecture-notes by Pt. Sanjay Rath <https://jyotish-blog.blogspot.com/2016/06/atri-03-class-navamsa-lecture-notes.html>

About The Author

Ajay Srivastava is the founder of lotuswisdom.in and holds 'Bachelor of Science' from Deen Dayal Upadhyay Gorakhpur University, Gorakhpur (UP) and 'Masters Programme in International Business' from PSG Institute of Management, Coimbatore (Tamil Nadu).

He has extensive experience in the capital market as a Lead Analyst, Investment Banker, Consultant, and Advisor in identifying investment opportunities and formulating strategies. In his career, he has written various research notes and has done in-depth research from a commercial and financing point of view in multiple deals. With diverse industry experience and wide understanding, he started imparting his knowledge in the industry since 2013.

He has deep knowledge of graphology and since childhood he is very much interested in analyzing a person by handwriting and has analyzed the handwriting of hundreds of persons in his life.

He is very much passionate to learn about astrology in deep and has completed 'JyotirVid' and 'JyotirVisharad' in Astrology from Bharatiya Vidya Bhavan, Mumbai. His various research articles have been published in the renowned magazine "The Astrological eMagazine".

Email ID: ajay.srivastava@lotuswisdom.in

Web Site: http://www.lotuswisdom.in/

Books Written by the Author

1. Psychology and Investment
2. Vedic Astrology: The Light of Wisdom
3. Midlife Crisis: An Astrological Appraoch
4. Jupiter: The Planet of Fortune
5. The Joy of Creation and Success
6. The Light of Nakshatras
7. Sun: The Supreme Creator
8. Astrology & Predictions
9. Animal Symbols of Nakshatras
10. Astrology & Profession
11. Rahu & Ketu: The Invisible & Mysterious Planets

Astrology Courses

1. Vedic Astrology for Beginners {Level – 1 (Basics)}

Module – 1: Basics of Astrology

Introduction; The Zodiac; Elements

Module – 2: Signs

Meaning of the Signs, Elements of the Signs, Qualities of the Signs, Odd and Even Signs, Sheershodaya & Prishtodaya Signs, Direction, Colors, Caste, Fruitful and Barren Signs, Masculine & Feminine Signs, Places, Other Major Qualities

Module – 3: Houses

Meaning of the 12 Houses, Types and Classifications of Houses

Module – 4: Planets

Planets and their Characteristics, Planetary Relationship, Exaltation, Debilitation & Mooltrikona, Natural Karakas, Karakas in Jaimini Astrology

Module – 5: Planets in Groups

Natural Benefic and Malefic Planets, Gender; Color; Caste; Guna and Places; Planet and Tastes; Nature of Planet; Elements; Metals; Age; Cloth and Height; Vegetable and Fruits; Physical Constituents and Tendency; Maturity Age of Planets; Planetary Aspects; Seasons; Hora

Module – 6: Planetary Strengths and Weaknesses

Strength of Planets based on its degrees, Direction; Direction Strength; Maran Karaka Sthana; Yog Karaka; Vargottam Planet; Shadabala

Module – 7: Retrograde and Combust Planet, Gandanta

2. <u>Vedic Astrology for Beginners {Level – 2 (Advanced)}</u>

Module 1: Vimshottari Dasha System

Nakshatra and Planetary Lordship, Change of Dasa and Results

Module 2: Basics of Nakshatra

Deity, Animal Symbol, Caste, Activity, Gana, Guna, Gender

Module 3: Important Yogas

Know the 30 most important astrological combinations

Module 4: Ashtakvarga

Interpretation of Ashtakvarga Table

Module 5: Transit of Planets and their impact

Understand the effect of transit of Jupiter, Saturn, Rahu-Ketu

Module 6: Planets and Profession

Identify the influence of the planet and the direction of profession

Module 7: Weak Planets and Remedies

Identify the signal of weak planets and useful remedies

Module 8: Key Steps to Chart Interpretation

Course Offerings:

- 30 hours of live sessions (Level 1 & Level 2)
- Learn various astrological concepts with practical examples
- Mode - Online Classes

3. Nakshatra Course

Knowledge of Nakshatra is very important in astrology, without it one cannot understand how energy works and what will be the result of the transit of planets. Do not limit yourself to the movement of planets, explore the world of Nakshatra and understand the hidden secrets.

What You'll Learn

- How the knowledge of Nakshatra helps to understand the characteristics and negative traits of the person
- Effect of transit of planets and time of activation
- Meaning of each symbol and its influence
- Influence of the associated animal on the personality of the person
- When to start a new venture and when not to go ahead
- Related Profession
- Understand each concept with logic

Course Offerings:

- 60 hours of live sessions
- Learn various astrological concepts with practical examples
- Mode - Online Classes, Recordings available
- Medium - English

Contact Us:

Mobile No.: +91 9867837184

Email ID: ajay.srivastava@lotuswisdom.in

Blog: https://lotuswisdomonline.blogspot.com/

4. A Course on Animal Symbols of Nakshatras

In the ancient scriptures, a total of 14 animals are related to the 27 nakshatras, and the behavior of every person is limited to these 14 animals. To understand the various merits and demerits of a person, it is necessary to understand the different characteristics of these animals.

How to Utilize Such Knowledge

- You will be surprised to know that these animals decide whom we form a relationship in our life.

- These animals determine our relationships with our friends, our spouse, our partners, our juniors and superiors.

- This knowledge helps to channelize your energy in pursuit of higher goals in life.

- The human mind is a very complex creation and it is difficult to say why a person behaves in a certain way and why his behavior changes. Knowledge of animal traits can provide proper guidance in this regard.

Course Offerings:

- 14 hours of live sessions

- Learn various astrological concepts with practical examples

- Mode - Online Classes; Recordings available

Sun:
The
Supreme
Creator
A Research Work on
Astrological Aspects of the Sun
Ajay Srivastava

The Light
of
Nakshatras
A Comprehensive Work to Explain the
Functioning of 27 Mystical Energies
Ajay Srivastava

Jupiter:
The
Planet of
Fortune
Ajay Srivastava

Vedic Astrology
The Light of Wisdom
Astrology for Beginners,
Learn the Language of Stars
Ajay Srivastava

Midlife
Crisis: An
Astrological
Approach
Understand The Timing Of Crisis,
Learn How To Turn A Crisis Into An Opportunity
Ajay Srivastava

PSYCHOLOGY
AND
INVESTMENT
The Art of Investing in Stocks with an
Explanation of Human Psychology
AJAY SRIVASTAVA

The Joy
of
Creation and Success
Ajay Srivastava

Astrology
&
Predictions
Ajay Srivastava

Animal Symbols
of
Nakshatras
Ajay Srivastava

Astrology
&
Profession
Astrological Principles Behind Career
Selection, Downfall and Resurrection
Ajay Srivastava

Rahu & Ketu
The Invisible and Mysterious Planets
An Extensive Research Work to Demystify
the Mystery of Lunar Nodes
Ajay Srivastava

Notes

www.ingramcontent.com/pod-product-compliance
Ingram Content Group UK Ltd.
Pitfield, Milton Keynes, MK11 3LW, UK
UKHW041313190726
13845UKWH00025B/228

9 789334 237023